Life With Sally
Little White Dog Tails

"I'm a confirmed cat person, or at least I was until I met Sally in person (in dog?) and read about her antics. She stares at toads, hauls around a garden rake like a giant bone, is afraid of thunder and hogs (dogs?) the bed. Oh, and she looks like a baby pig. Tricia L. McDonald is smitten with this little dervish, and when you read Life With Sally, *you will be, too."*
     - ELLE MADISON, author of *Mental*

*"*Life with Sally *stories are a look into a life with a happy, silly dog. They remind us why we treasure dogs as much as we do. They make you want to give your dog an extra hug too!"*
     - TONYA CHRISTIANSEN - Owner of Must Love Dogs Boutique & Spa

"A little white dog with an oversized personality, Sally rockets through life, terrorizing lawn rakes, stepping out in her new shoes, and spinning in circles. With affection and more than a touch of humor, author Tricia McDonald explores the bond between owner and pet in Life With Sally. *Readers will be reminded of the lesson that pets teach so well, that life, in all its big and small moments, is meant to be enjoyed."*
     - SARAH McELRATH—Library Media Specialist, GHAPS

sally

What does Sally
love to lick? pg 91

Life With Sally
Little White Dog Tails

Tricia by McD

Tricia L. McDonald

Writers Avenue, LLC
Michigan

Life With Sally
Little White Dog Tails

by Tricia L. McDonald

First Printing: November 2009

ISBN-13 978-0-615-32950-5

Published by:

Writers Avenue, LLC
17190 Van Wagoner Road
Spring Lake, MI 49456

Orders at www.awritingpassage.com

Printed in the United States of America

Dedicated to my muse … Sally.

Acknowledgments

In thanking everyone who has helped in the creation of this book, I have to start with my little white dog, Sally, for providing me with a plethora of story ideas. And for turning me into a Sally person.

And of course, if it weren't for Janet Vormittag's encouragement to write the *Life With Sally* column, none of this would be happening.

Thanks to my son, Jacob Kubon, who is the graphics artist extraordinaire, and a constant supporting force.

To Mike, my husband, who has been fodder for many of the stories and never complained, although I did get "the look" once in awhile. My daughter, Nicole Kubon, for listening to me ramble on ad nausea about Sally.

Thank you to Ellen Hosafros who was always there to fight my gremlins for me.

To my writing friends, writing groups and Peninsula Writers who helped me by work-shopping the various stories, and laughing!

To my family and friends, who have encouraged this endeavor.

And everyone who has taken the time to tell me how much they love the Sally stories, either in person or by e-mail.

This has been an amazing journey and I thank you all!

Table of Contents

Change of Heart

Flight 5689 lands with Sally, a little white dog, in its cargo area. After months of negotiations, only a desk separates me from my first meeting with that dog.

I shift from foot to foot at the check-in counter as the clerk on the other side stares at a computer screen. I cough into my hand, but her eyes don't move. I clear my throat and smile. Her brow furrows as she hits keys in rapid succession.

Behind her, a man in an airline uniform bangs through the door carrying three pet carriers. As he drops them on the non-moving conveyor belt, loud meowing emanates from two of them. The other is silent.

The clerk continues her typing and frowning.

"Excuse me," I say.

She lifts her chin, never taking her eyes off the screen. I lean closer to the counter and cock my head, trying to see what has her so captivated. She turns it away from me. "Yes?"

"I'm here to pick up my puppy." I point toward the quiet carrier. "I think she's in there."

"Name?"

"Sally."

"Last name."

"What? I guess it would be McDonald."

Her fingers hit the keys. "We don't have any information for a Sally McDonald."

"Oh, no. That's the dog's name." I chuckle. She doesn't. I clear my throat and start rambling. "My husband's favorite movie is *When Harry Met Sally*. Since we already had a Harry, it only made sense that this puppy would be a Sally." I smile again. "So I thought you were asking for, never mind."

She stares at me, her hands poised in space above the keyboard.

"Tricia," I say. "Tricia McDonald."

She hits a few keys, a ticket spits out of a machine, and she turns to match it to the carriers.

"I think it's the one not meowing," I say. She continues checking the tags, then places the carrier on the counter. The opening is facing away from me.

"Okay, that will be $180.19 for the flight," she says. I hand her my credit card as I peek through the slits in the carrier.

"Do you think you could turn that around?" I ask. "I've never seen her before."

She nudges the carrier into a half turn with her elbow, and I see a little pinkish-white snout and bright black eyes looking at me.

Sally, our miniature bull terrier, is for my husband, Mike. Five months earlier we had lost nine-year old Harry, our border terrier, to cancer. Harry and Mike had a bond I didn't understand, because I am not a dog person. As a cat person, I see dogs differently.

Dog tongues are often coated with dirt, drool or even unmentionables, so doggy kisses make me gag. Dogs enjoy getting muddy and dirty. And they don't groom themselves; they just get muddier. Sometimes they roll in dead or rotting things. They jump, dirtying your pants or ruining your pantyhose. They are loud, and they bark and bark, never knowing when to shut up. They often mistake a litter box for a snack box. And without fail they always need to go outside in the middle of the night during a snow or rain storm.

It wasn't that I didn't love Harry. It just wasn't the same love Mike had for that little dog. Harry had taken his last breath in Mike's arms. Though it had been months, I could still see the pain of his death in Mike's eyes.

I was sad, but Mike grieved. He wept when he walked in the door after work and Harry was not there to greet him. He sat alone in his recliner, leaving the spot next to him, where Harry used to sit, vacant. I tried to warm the place in bed between us where Harry had slept, but it still felt cold.

My heart was heavy with Mike's grief, and I wanted to find a way to help him through his pain. I broached the idea of a new dog. I thought a dog, not a replacement for Harry, would help Mike.

"Why don't we get a puppy?" I said.

Tears sprang to his eyes. "Not yet."

Then a month later he told me about a bull terrier kennel he had found on the internet. Mike had been attracted to the bull terrier breed for years. Me, not so much. In fact, I found them to be ugly! I saw long snouts, beady black eyes, and egg-shaped heads, along with big, muscular bodies. If we were going to get another dog, I was hoping for something small and snuggly. Mike told me these puppies were miniatures, which I thought would help with the small factor. I still couldn't see a bull terrier as snuggly, even a small one. But the puppy was for Mike, and it was time.

I checked out the puppy photos online. They were pretty cute, but most puppies are, even to non-dog people. I contacted the breeder and asked if the white bully (Mike's favorite) was a female. She was. And, she was ready for adoption. We were getting a new puppy for Mike!

"Here is your card back," the clerk says. "And I need a signature."

I tear my eyes away from the carrier and sign the paperwork. She pushes the carrier toward me, I lift it off the counter and put it on the floor.

As I open the front latch, a little pig-like puppy jumps out. Her short fur is white, barely concealing her pink damp skin. *Why are you wet?* I think, until I hold her close to my face and smell a distinct sour odor. I hold her away from me. She wiggles and sticks her tiny tongue at my face. I pull back and squint, my eyes assaulted by the scent of puppy pee. She licks the air.

It is early December in Michigan, with a light covering of snow on the ground. Sally has flown in from the warmer weather of Kentucky.

With excitement, I set her down near a tree for her first experience with the cold, white stuff. She tugs at a dead root sticking out of the ground, pulling with great intensity and shaking her little head back and forth. When the ground releases the root, she lands with a thump on her backside. Then she is off, running circles around the tree with the root in her mouth.

I laugh out loud as she runs to me, stopping too late and sliding into my leg. I feel her shiver as I pick her up and tuck her inside my coat. There she snuggles against my body, and into my heart.

Fur Abounds

"Sally, leave the cat alone."

Stanley, our very large five-year-old feline, is sprawled on his side in the living room with Sally looming over him. There is no movement from Stanley, other than a slight flipping of his tail. Of course, this speaks volumes, as in, this little white dog is harassing him again.

Hanging off the chair beside them is Socks. He is Stan's littermate, although their only common characteristics are bellies that sway back and forth when they walk. Stan's short fur is black and white, while Socks is gray. The first time we saw them they were six weeks old and in a cage with three other siblings at the local humane society. When we left the building, they left with us.

Sally leaps off Stan in a backward jump. Stan continues to lay still, but for the tail flipping. Sally crouches, readying for another attack when Socks swats at her wiggling back end. Sally turns, looks at her own tail and the spinning begins. As Sally's spinning becomes more erratic, Stan turns tail and dashes out of the room. Socks watches from the safety of his chair, his head moving in a circular motion as he watches Sally chase her own tail.

Sally is smaller than both of the cats, by about five pounds. Yet the difference in size does not stop her from being the aggressor in their play. It has gotten to the point where the cats will just drop over when Sally walks up to them. Playing dead seems to be the strategy.

Then there is Louis, our three-year-old cat. Another shelter rescue, his striped brown coat and sleek body is a huge contrast to the fatty cattys. He also has a proud, long tail that he holds straight in the air, similar to a flag on a dune buggy. We always know where Louis is when the tail cruises past.

Louis ambles into the room and Sally stops spinning. Louis meows and Sally drops to the floor on her belly, in stealth attack mode. Louis walks by, pausing to give a look of disdain toward this little pig-like puppy, then continues his stride. Sally's breathing is labored as she continues watching Louis, her head the only thing moving as she follows the Louis stroll. When Louis walks out of the room, Sally rises into a half-crawl position and sneaks along the wall. She peeks around the edge at Louis, and then drops back into the stealth attack mode again.

Louis wanders into our bedroom, the end of that flag-like tail flipping in the air. Sally crawls to the bedroom and drops again. Peeking around the door, she springs into action, running into the room and sliding sideways under the bed. Louis is on top of the bed, making kitty biscuits into the blankets.

I decide it is time for a distraction.

"Sally, let's go outside."

The *outside* word springs her into action, and her nails scrabble on the hardwood floor as she wiggles out from under the bed. She gives Louis one last longing look, then bounces to the back door. I hear Mary, our five year-old lab/cocker mix, jump off the couch and join Sally.

After Harry, our border terrier, died, Mary went into a doggy depression. When outdoors, she would walk to the end of the driveway, lie down with her head on her paws and stay that way until we called her back inside. We tried to distract her by throwing her tennis ball, but she would just watch us, her head on her paws. Her beautiful red coat started to dull, and her grief was palpable.

Sally's arrival changed all that. Mary no longer sulks on the driveway and her obsessive ball chasing has returned. She and Sally don't seem to be buddies, though. Most of the time Mary looks annoyed that Sally is around. She seems to tolerate her existence, even though it is obvious that Sally's presence helped bring her out of her depression.

After a number of "sit stills," I manage to get collars on both of the wiggling dogs and open the door. They run through the garage and into the white wonderland of a Michigan winter. Mary leaps over a snow bank, and Sally runs along the edge of the driveway until she finds a place short enough to climb over. Jumping into the fluffy whiteness, she hops after Mary, the air exploding around her with snowflakes. Mary turns and eggs her on, waiting until she gets close before bounding through the drifts.

"Come on girls, let's go this way," I call as I head down the deserted road. They run ahead. Mary is a streak of red fur, with Sally, her stubby white pig-like body following behind.

A few minutes in, Sally turns and runs back to me. I crouch and she puts her front paws on my knee. I pick her up and tuck her inside my coat. She peeks out as I continue walking, but it doesn't take long before she tucks her little white snout inside.

Around me the snowflakes fall and I feel the chill in the air. But inside my coat, a little white dog snuggles in and falls asleep.

First Day of Puppy School

"What should I wear?" I ask my husband.

"To what?"

"Tonight is Sally's first puppy class!"

I toss a pair of jeans on the bed. Casual, won't show the dirt, but bending in them makes my middle a bit uncomfortable. Now, what to wear with them? Blouse or shirt? Tucked or un-tucked? Sweatshirt or sweater? Dressy or casual? I'm deciding between several ensembles laid out on the bed when my son Jake walks in.

"What's up?" he asks, munching on a bag of chips.

"I'm trying to decide what to wear to puppy class."

"You're kidding. It's puppy class, mom," he says, shaking his head. "Get it? Puppy. It's about the puppy."

"I know, I know," I say. "But ..."

Embarrassed by the absurdity of what I'm doing and being called out on it, I grab my sweatshirt and jeans and head for the bathroom. "Okay, okay, I got it."

He chuckles and pats me on the shoulder. "You'll be alright, Mom."

Once I'm dressed, I help Sally into her dark green knitted sweater. She only has one so there are no fashion decisions to be made.

"Mom, she looks ridiculous in that thing," Jake says, throwing a toy for her. She runs after it, stops halfway and starts pulling on the sweater string.

"She looks adorable."

"I can't believe you've become one of those people who dress their pets."

I ignore his sarcasm. "She gets cold outside."

"Just look at her, she hates it." He picks her up and pulls the soggy string out of her mouth. "Ugh!" She nips at his nose with her razor-like puppy teeth and he hands her over to me. I bend to put her down and the button on my jeans pops.

We arrive at puppy class two minutes late. Sally has managed to pull her sweater halfway over her head. Hanging over her eyes, she weaves down the sidewalk to the building.

Through the windows I can see the other puppies and owners sitting on chairs along the wall. The owners sit straight, their attire clean and pressed, no strands of hair out of place. I look down and notice a Taco Bell mild sauce stain on my sweatshirt.

The puppies lay at their owners' feet. There is hardly a movement in the room. The scene freaks me out.

Someone should make a movie out of this and call it Stepford Dogs.

Sally turns to chew on her leash while I try to open the door without dropping the paperwork, the bag of treats and my purse. Meanwhile, Sally's spit-covered leash is wrapped around and through my legs. Instead of walking into the room, I fall in.

I scramble to my feet. Inside, Carol, the instructor, wearing a small microphone attached to the collar of her starched shirt, greets us. She stands at attention, similar to a Marine drill sergeant, with her hands clasped behind her back. Nodding at me, she glances at the clock, and then the check-in table. I wonder if I can blame Sally if I pee on the floor right now.

I give Carol the paperwork and drag Sally across the room where I collapse on a folding chair. She's chewing on the leash and tugging against me, shaking her head in a death-grip. Is she growling? I drop my purse and bag of puppy treats next to me, and untangle the leash from around my ankles, again. Sally takes this opportunity to drop her end of the leash and grab the treat bag, pulling it to the floor. I bend to pick it up, the back of the chair tips and I end up on the cold, and I'm sure previously peed on by every type of dog imaginable, cement floor.

The crashing startles the other puppies. The German shepherd starts barking and the golden retriever hides under a chair. Sally doesn't notice, or care, because her face is buried in a pile of Snausages.

"Sorry," I mumble, as I push Sally away from the treats and scoop them back into the bag. I sit down and pick her up, hiding my scarlet face in her soft white neck, wondering whose idea this class was, anyway.

We get through the first lesson without anymore mishaps, and I beam with pride when Sally sits with little prompting. It appears she is a natural at this stuff, and I can tell she is the smartest dog in class, even if she isn't from Stepford.

The second lesson is the down command. According to Carol, first I have to get Sally to lie down with a treat. Then she gets the treat after she lies down, and finally, I name the behavior (down) and she does it. Since Sally is the smartest dog in class, this should be a breeze.

A tiny problem presents itself— Sally doesn't lie down. Maybe the floor is too cold, maybe she's distracted by the other dogs, or maybe she just doesn't feel like listening to me. Whatever her reason, she refuses to lie down. She sits, she stands, and she spins in a circle. She does every contortion known to man and dog, but she will NOT lie down. So while Carol, who's obviously trying not to roll her eyes, and the rest of the class member, who are rolling theirs, are moving on to step two, and then step three, I'm still begging Sally to accomplish step one.

Carol senses my frustration and walks over to lend her expertise. Seems she also has better treats, because Sally is happy to stay right next to her. Carol offers her a liver snack and moves her hand to the down position. Sally does an impressive somersault, but no down. Despite repeated attempts, an array of treats, and many, many minutes, Sally refuses.

The first class and my humiliation end and I gather my purse and empty treat bag. I snap the leash back on Sally's collar and begin to notice the effects of too many treats. Sally is wagging her tail while I wave my hand in front of my nose.

"Just keep working with Sally this week on the down command," Carol offers. She waves her hand in front of her nose, too.

The golden retriever owner walks past and tells me not to worry, he's sure Sally will come around, eventually. He looks doubtful, though.

"Come on, Sally," I say, tugging at her leash.

We hurry to the door. The leash tangles around my ankles and down I go.

A Doggy Massage

"You are not going to believe what Sally did yesterday," I say to my friend Janet.

Janet has started *Cats and Dogs, A Magazine Devoted to Companion Animals.* I have been writing articles for her and we are having our weekly breakfast meeting.

"You should write a column about Sally for the magazine," Janet says.

"Yeah, right. Who would want to read about my silly little dog?"

But the seed was planted and the next month was the debut of "Life With Sally." After all, other than living with Sally, what could be more fun than writing about her?

My first interview for the "Life with Sally" column is with a canine massager. As I pack up to go, I grab Sally's collar from the doggie hook in the kitchen, and she begins her going-for-a-ride frenzy: a tail-chasing dizzying dervish of white fur, clicking toe nails and wet tongue. It takes a few minutes, but I catch her and secure the collar. She bounds to the car and we are off.

We meet the doggy masseuse at Must Love Dogs, a dog boutique in Grand Haven, Michigan, where she has volunteered to give canine massages, donating the proceeds to a local humane society.

Sally is first in line to receive a massage. The masseuse hefts Sally's 25 pounds of muscled body onto the massage table. The first thing the masseuse does is ask Sally if she wants a massage. Sally jerks her head in what appears to be an enthusiastic smile. I am happy she doesn't clip the masseuse on the chin with that rock-like head of hers. I have been on the receiving end of those enthusiastic head-butts, which often resulted in me biting my tongue.

The masseuse's hands move lightly across Sally's

short white fur and down each leg. Meanwhile, Sally watches the door as people come in and out, keeping an eye on Pumpkin, a Basenji/Whippet who is also in the store. Sally stares at me adoringly. Okay, maybe I am doing the stare of adoration.

When she finishes, the masseuse thanks Sally and puts her on the floor. The massage seems to have energized her and she runs up to everyone coming and going, ricocheting off their legs while Mike and I sing a chorus of "Stay down, Sally!"

We check out the doggie clothing attire in the dog friendly store. I hold up a pink fur-lined jacket and a hooded chocolate brown sweatshirt, to which Mike gives a thumbs-down. He doesn't want her to wear anything too girly. After all, she is a lean muscle machine!

I pull a black and white Al Poochtee Spotface (Scarface) t-shirt over Sally's head, and the choice is no longer ours. Sally spins her dance of approval. Mike forks over the money for the outfit, and we are off.

Once in the car, Sally turns twice in a tight circle, folds herself onto my lap, and within a few blocks, she is sound asleep. There is no interest in looking out the window on the drive home. Her morning out has exhausted her.

At home, Sally jumps out of the car and runs up to Jake. He shakes his head and eyes me with a mixture of sympathy and wonder.

"Since when did you become one of those people who dress their dog?" he asks.

"You've already asked me that question," I say.

I smile as I watch Sally hop up and down through the snow drifts in her new shirt.

"But I guess it was when I became a Sally person."

The Giant Needle

"Look at the size of that needle!" I stammer.

Sally, Mike and I are standing in the waiting room at the local humane society. A kennel technician holds a thick, gigantic hypodermic needle to his side, away from Sally. His behavior reminds me of when I would take my children (now 21 and 23 years old) to the pediatrician for an injection. The doctor hid the needle from sight until the last moment.

And now my eyes are riveted to this needle that seems to grow larger as I watch. I feel a little sick.

"Some owners don't want to be in the room when we microchip their pet," Tech Guy says, reading the horror that has rearranged my face. He explains that the needle has to be large to accommodate the microchip, which is about the size of a grain of rice. It amazes me that this tiny microchip contains a one-of-a-kind identification number that will be unique to Sally.

Sally is 25 pounds of muscle and as solid as a

doggie bodybuilding contestant. The toughness stops with her appearance. Really -- and I say this with complete love -- she is a total wimp. After dark, while squatting to take care of her business in our backyard, she scans the woods behind our house as if she is preparing to run in the opposite direction of whatever is lurking there. "Guard dog" is not in her job description.

She's just as wary when we take her for walks. We live at the end of a dead-end road that winds through the woods. It's a nice walk to the mailbox at the end of our dirt two-track.

On one occasion, Mike and I were walking the dogs when Sally heard a noise. It might have been a neighbor's dog barking, or a leaf falling from a tree, or the rustle of my windbreaker. Whatever she heard, she didn't like it. She spun around and dashed back home, leaving a dust trail behind her. We found her sitting on the stoop in the garage, staring bug-eyed at the door and shivering with fear.

It occurred to me how frightened she would be if she became lost in the wide expanse of woods surrounding our home, or if she dashed away from me in town. What's more, it would drive Mike and I crazy thinking about her wandering around alone without us to protect her.

That's how my adorable little wimp ended up in the treatment room, wagging her tail, unaware that she is about to be stabbed with the micro-chip needle. Sally is busy sniffing at the cracks under the doors and winding her leash around everyone's legs. I, on the other hand, still can't take my eyes off the enormous needle. I wipe the sweat from my forehead and ask a million questions. How long does the chip last?

For the life of your pet.

Does the chip ever migrate in the body?

Rarely, but it won't hurt the dog and that is why we scan the whole body when a lost animal turns up here.

Does a pet have to be a certain age to be micro-chipped?

No, pets of any age can be injected with the microchip.

It is time to get down to business. A surgical assistant holds Sally with a firm, yet gentle, hand. I stroke Sally's long nose as the assistant nuzzles her head. With the ease of someone who has performed this action many,

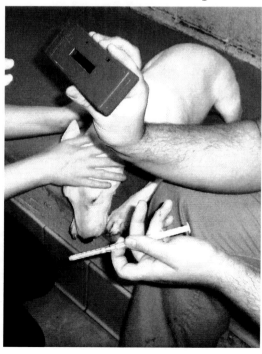 many times, Tech Guy slides the g a r g a n t u a n needle into the pink skin between Sally's shoulder blades. I hold my breath and wait for her to jerk away, twist her head toward the invading creature, yelp in pain … something.

She does nothing. I have

seen more of a reaction when a fly landed on her back and she went into one of her tail-chasing spins.

It is done. I run my hand along the injection spot, feeling for the microchip, but I can detect nothing. Tech Guy runs the hand-held scanner across Sally's back and her identification number lights up like a lighthouse beacon on a dark night. Mike and I high-five each other. Now if Sally is ever separated from us, she has permanent identification that cannot be lost, altered or removed, unlike a simple collar.

It is time to go home. The barking from the kennels has moved my dog-loving Mike to the point of tears and turned Sally into a trembling ball of nerves. They escape to the car while I fill out the requisite paperwork. As I read, I learn the microchip is only as good as the information it contains. A pet owner must take care to change contact information following a move. Too many micro-chipped pets remain separated from their families because phone numbers and addresses haven't been updated.

As I open the door to join Mike and Sally in the car, I see her standing with her front paws against the dashboard, her tongue smearing doggie-spit on the windshield. Her excitement at seeing me warms my heart, and knowing she is now protected with a microchip should we ever be separated gives me a sense of peace.

No Splashing Allowed

Splashing, running and jumping are what you'd associate with kids and the summer opening of a community pool. Only the children in this setting are furry and four-legged, and the pool is a pond at Shaggy Pines Dog Park, a 20-acre private park, located in Michigan.

Not that any of this matters to Sally. She stands between my feet, almost yawning with indifference at the antics of the other dogs. Sally is not the swimming or wading type. She loves the hose and is happy to be sprayed with the different nozzle attachments. And watering the garden proves to be dangerous for the flowers, because Sally unknowingly will destroy plants while attacking the water. But standing bodies of water – nope, she doesn't want anything to do with them.

The dogs at Shaggy Pines are jumping and running into the pond. They chase each other, their tails, or balls thrown by their owners. The pond is a frenetic, churning caldron of ears and tails. A 6-month-old dark brown labradoodle named Gidget runs by, chasing a goldendoodle, 2-year-old Lloyd. A German shepherd puppy runs in circles around the perimeter, getting his feet wet but not much else. Sally stands and stares.

My daughter Nicole is visiting from college and has joined us. She picks up a stick.

"Sally," she says. Sally perks up at the stick as Nicole waves it in front of her.

"Go get it." Nicole throws the stick in the water.

Sally makes a movement toward the water, but she is cut off by a Malamute headed for the same stick. Sally sits down and watches as the dog swims out to the stick, retrieves it and takes it to its owner on the other side of the pond.

Nicole gives me a pathetic look. "Sally's a weird dog."

"Maybe she's just overwhelmed," I say, feeling the need to defend Sally's lack of dogness. "Let's take her for a walk."

We head toward the woods outside the Shaggy Pines building, passing several more dogs. A ripple of "new kid" goes through the animals when they spy Sally. Five dogs rush up to her and start sniffing every inch of her as she backs up, trying to get away. We move toward the walkway through the woods, where Sally is no longer the center of attention. Now free of the curiosity of other dogs, she runs along the hiking trail with an occasional glance behind her.

We explore the different trails, then return to the pond and try to urge Sally into the water. No go. She seems more interested in the owners than the dogs, and they in her. Running up to people with her tail wagging, she teases them with a moment of petting, then she runs to the next person. My daughter keeps shaking her head at me, and I hear her mutter that I have turned Sally into a non-dog.

"She's a dog!" I reply.

Now Mike is shaking his head at me, too.

"So she doesn't like to run head-first into a muddy pond with other dogs that are three times her size. Doesn't that sound a little smart? And so what if she doesn't chase your normal dog objects like tennis balls and sticks. She does like to chase lacrosse balls."

"Mom, settle down," Nicole says.

"And so what if she has a tireless obsession with rakes, brooms and shovels. Doesn't that just make her unique?" I stop short of discussing her attention deficit disorder and obsessive compulsive disorder tendencies. Better to stop while I am ahead.

We spend another hour walking, meeting other dogs on the trails, and Sally, to Nicole's amazement and my satisfaction, starts playing with Lloyd. She jumps at his face with reckless abandon while Lloyd rolls on his back. It is hard to tell whether he is playing or trying to dry off after his numerous trips into the pond.

Several days later, Jake joins me when I take Sally to another dog park with two ponds. We visit on a weekday, and we are the only people there, other than the regular borders and day-care doggies. Sally, Jake and I set off on one of the trails that leads to the first pond. Sally runs up to the edge and walks in, lapping at the water. My mouth falls open. Jake starts snapping photos.

"After what happened at Shaggy Pines, I can't believe she's in the water," I say.

Jake takes off his shoes and socks, steps into the pond and coaxes Sally. She is having nothing to do with it.

Jake takes off running around the edge of the pond, with Sally hot on his heels, that silly constant smile on her face. She is running in the water but staying in the very shallow edge. Jake runs around a curve in the pond and Sally cuts the corner. Without warning she is in water up to her neck! She comes to a dead stop, seeming to question how this has happened and doesn't waste any time paddling toward the shore. That is the end of her pond swimming for the day. I can't wait to go home and call Nicole to tell her – somewhat smugly – that Sally had indeed acted like a dog.

Make Mine A Cone

"I scream, you scream, we all scream for ice cream." Well, not exactly. It is more like "I *bark*, you *bark*, we all *bark* for ice cream."

It is Saturday, and we decide to take a trip so Sally can visit Cones and Bones, an ice cream parlor in Lansing, Michigan that caters to dogs and people. Mike suggests the trip, and Jake agrees to come along to take photos. Pulling onto the road, I question the common sense behind a 3-hour drive just so Sally can have ice cream.

"Maybe I should just take her to the local ice cream store instead," I say.

"Do they have ice cream for dogs?" Mike asks.

"They have a doggy sundae, but Cones and Bones is specifically for dogs."

Since we don't have anything else planned that day, Mike insists we head to Lansing. I should have paid attention to my intuition.

Sally is restless. She spends the drive climbing

from the backseat with Jake to my lap in the front seat. Mike spends the trip trying to block her attempts with his arm and telling her to lie down. Jake spreads a towel for her, but she paws at it until it moves out of her way.

"What's that smell?" Jake asks, fanning his face. "Is that you or Sally?"

No one responds.

"He's not talking to me," I say to Mike.

"What? It's not me who made that smell" Mike says.

We both turn and look in the backseat. Sally grins back at us.

Passing gas is a common occurrence during Sally's car rides, probably due to excitement. She never appears to be in distress, but those around her are.

Jake rolls the window down to clear the smell, and Sally lunges across his lap to stick out her head. She tangles herself in the strings of his headphones, and when she backs away, they pop out of his ears.

Mike realizes the directions from the Internet are wrong. Tension in the car starts to rise. I call Cones and Bones and we learn that we should have turned east, not west. We turn the car around while Jake gets Sally settled onto the seat beside him, and within minutes we are pulling into the parking lot.

The place is full of people and dogs. It is divided by wall-sized windows and a door, serving dogs on one side and people on the other. With Sally leading the way, we enter the dog side of Cones and Bones. Once inside, we are greeted by owner Jim Byrnes, as well as a Burmese mountain dog on his way out, and Marcus, a 9-week-old

Chihuahua, on his way in.

The doggy ice cream on the menu is designed for diabetic and lactose-intolerant people. Dog customers have their choice of three sizes of ice cream: The Chihuahua (small), The Labrador (medium) or The Great Dane (large).

After the gas-passing incident on our trip here, we order the Chihuahua for Sally. The ice cream is served in a plastic bowl with bits of doggie bones crumbled onto the top. Although distracted by Marcus, who is nibbling at his ice cream nearby, it doesn't take long before Sally is nose-deep in her own bowl.

When she finishes, Sally lets out an impressive belch while Mike wipes at her chin. Before we leave, Byrnes takes her picture to add to the hundreds of doggie customer photos on the walls.

I walk next door and order an Amaretto ice cream
in a waffle cone for me (no one else is interested in ice
cream), and we all pile back into the car.

Within minutes, Jake has his earphones back on,
Mike has us headed in the right direction, and I am
licking away at my Amaretto. And how is Sally after her
first ice cream treat? She is sacked out on her side,
snoring happily.

The best part of the day is that she manages not to
gas us on the way home.

A Week Without Sally

"Hi Sally!" I whisper into my cell phone. "How's my girl?"

Silence. What did I expect? A little whine of recognition or maybe a bark? That would have been nice.

"Sorry, Mom. She's distracted," Jake says from the other end of the line. "She's just looking for the cat again. She's been stalking Louis all day."

I slump onto my bed. I am attending a weeklong writing retreat; a week of writing, beautiful weather, a great speaker and the opportunity to interact with other writers. Blissful! It is also a week of no laundry, no television, no work schedule and ... uh oh, no Sally. A week without Sally? What was I thinking?

The first day started with the three-hour drive to Villa Glen, in Northern Michigan, followed by unpacking and settling into my cottage. The sun was shining and I spent several hours sitting outside reading. Not a bad way to pass a summer day. About 10 p.m. I headed toward bed with a book, and I automatically looked around for Sally.

Our bedtime routine at home goes like this: Sally is already there, snuggled into the pillows. If she's not, I call, "Sally, are you ready for bed?" and she runs into the bedroom, crouches down on the rug, wiggles her butt, then leaps onto the bed. Once there she runs back and forth in a maniacal Terrier-tear while the pillows fly onto the floor.

After she calms down, I read my book while she chews on a bone. Several minutes later, the bone and book are put into the nightstand, the lights are shut off and we snuggle in the blankets. Sally has a whole different routine with my husband when he comes to bed, which, he tells me, includes obsessive face licking, but by then I'm sound asleep.

And now my first night at the retreat and there is no Sally to snuggle against. I don't have my husband to snuggle either, and I really miss him too, but we're talking about Sally here.

I hold off for several days and then call home. My son answers the phone and I ask to talk to Sally. He heaves a weary sigh and calls her to the phone.

I am concerned about how my roommates will react to me talking to my dog on the phone, so I walk into my bedroom, close the door, and speak in a whisper. I needn't have worried about their response. The next night my roommate walks into the room talking on her cell phone. She is explaining to her husband the location of the speaker button on the phone he is holding. Once that is established, her voice takes on an excited tone as she speaks to her dog.

"It's momma!" she coos. "Are you a good girl? Yes, you are. You're momma's goooooooooood girl." She presses her lips against the cell phone and plants several wet kisses.

I miss Sally even more.

On the last day of the retreat, I head out first thing in the morning, anxious to get home. I am excited to see Sally! As I pull into the driveway, I see my husband mowing the lawn and Mary running around the yard, but no Sally. My husband receives a big hug before I head for the front door.

"I'll let her out," Mike says, rolling his eyes. He walks to the door and opens it. A white ball of muscle comes flying down the stairs and straight toward me. I bend down to her level, and she never veers, slams right into me and knocks me onto my butt. This gives her the

perfect position to cover me with excited licks, combined with jumping and spinning into the air.

"You think she missed you?" Mike says.

Holding her is out of the question. She runs around me in circles, tears across the yard, then back again, and spins around in her obsessive compulsive disorder way of expressing happiness. I, in my way of expressing happiness, can't stop smiling and laughing at her antics.

Later that night, I change into my pajamas and pick up my book.

"Sally, ready for bed?" But she is already curled into the pillows, waiting for her bone, our bedtime routine and me.

My week without Sally is over.

Don't Make Me Get Wet

I wrestle the kiddie pool onto the deck, turn on the hose and watch as the clear shimmering water flows.

Sally stands with her head cocked, watching the giant blue water bowl. The Michigan days have been hot, with temperatures of 80 to 90 degrees, for over a week with no relief in sight. Doggie pools are very popular with the doggie daycare society, and I am excited for Sally to be a part of that crowd. Plus, the pool will provide a cool reprieve from the scorching heat.

As the pool fills, Sally and Mary run off to find something more interesting. Sally discovers a sunny spot in the grass and rolls onto her back, wriggling back and forth. Mary drops her ball next to me. Her eyes dart between my face and the ball, back and forth in a maniacal frenzy. I toss it into the woods, and she runs after it like a speeding bullet.

I slide my feet into the icy, yet refreshing, water.

"Sally, come get in the pool," I call. During an

earlier trip to a local doggie pond, Sally had been reluctant to play in the water.

Sally jumps up from her back-wiggling position and dashes up the stairs. Yes! I was worried that with her idiosyncrasies, she would not like the pool. My excitement is short-lived as she skids to a stop when I move my toes and the water ripples. I coax her to me and pour some of the water onto her snout. She stands as still as a statue.

"This is going to be so much fun!" I say.

She barely moves.

I pick her up and place her in the water with me. You would think I placed her in a vat of wet concrete. She doesn't budge. I pour more water over her back, and she remains a dog statue. Mary has now abandoned her tennis ball and is watching Sally. I'm sure I notice her shaking her head with sympathy.

What is wrong with this picture? Dogs love water, right? Sally isn't too keen on the ponds at the dog parks, but I attribute that to the splashing, depth of the water and the frenetic activity of the other dogs.

There is no splashing here. No depth problem, either. The water is barely over her paws. Sally inches her way out of the pool, and I shake my head.

Time to bring out the arsenal. I hold a doggie treat over the water. She stretches her stubby bull terrier neck as far as she can until she reaches the treat without getting back in the pool. We do this several times, and then I drop the treat in the middle. She runs around several times, puts one front paw into the pool, and then the next. She pokes, notice I don't say <u>plunges</u>, her long white nose into the water. But she hasn't held her breath, and she starts sputtering. She does this a few more times until she reaches the treat. Success!

We continue this way throughout the afternoon, and she does put all four paws into the water. But she never looks like she is having fun.

The next day I throw Mary's tennis ball into the pool, and she jumps in, plunging her reddish-brown nose in the water and comes out with the ball. Aha! I throw Sally's lacrosse ball into the pool and get excited when she runs to the edge. She stops, lifts each leg and places it into the pool. Standing in the water, she puts her snout into the water, again forgetting to hold her breath, but she manages to retrieve the ball. When Mary jumps in while Sally is in the pool, Sally turns away and squints from the splashing.

The problem is not water; Sally loves the garden hose. I learn this while watering my flower garden. She jumps into the flowerbed trying to catch the spray of

water in her mouth.

She leaps at the stream and chomps at the water. She twirls, runs back and forth chasing the flow, and accomplishes some acrobatic moves that are amazing. By the time I shut the hose off, she is dripping wet.

And water is water, whether it is in a pool or being sprayed from a hose, right? Not according to Sally.

Sally & the Pet Psychic

Sally has this weird thing with our cat Louis. He is a four-year-old brown tabby with a long tail, which he always holds straight up, like a flag on a dune buggy.

Sally stalks Louis. She follows him throughout the house, peeking around corners at him. She will crouch under the coffee table, as if no one can see her, especially Louis. If Louis trots to the bedroom, Sally runs in and slides sideways under the bed with the dust bunnies. It's bizarre behavior since Sally doesn't do that with the other cats.

Socks and Stan, our other two cats, are nine-year-old littermates who are almost as wide as they are long. When Sally passes them, they just fall over. Or they rub up against her long snout, often when she's in a Louis-trance. Sally doesn't stalk them.

This behavior always mystified us, so when a pet psychic was coming to visit Sally, it was one of the questions we were hoping to get answered. What was it about Louis that fascinated Sally? Or repelled her?

I don't know what I am expecting when the pet psychic steps out of her car in our driveway, but it isn't the petite woman wearing a black pantsuit. In my limited experience with psychics (i.e. none), I had developed a stereotype of a woman wearing a long, flowing dress, with lots of rings and silver bracelets. I am so wrong. This woman laughs when she realizes her black pants will be covered in white Sally fur by the time she leaves. She is warm, friendly, intelligent and most important, Sally loves her.

When they meet, Sally goes into a spinning frenzy and runs back and forth between the pet psychic and myself.

After the introductions, the pet psychic sits cross-legged on the floor next to Sally's pillow. She closes her eyes and meditates. Sally goes into a flurry of activity. She jumps into the pet psychic's lap and rolls around. She jumps out of the lap, runs to her pillow, then back to the psychic and starts licking her face. Then back into her lap. Mind you, I am sitting on the floor across from the psychic, yet Sally never comes to me. It is as if there is a silent conversation going on, and I am not invited to participate.

A few minutes into the session, Sally sits very still on her pillow and stares at the psychic's face. She doesn't wiggle or look around the room; she settles into the pillow and keeps staring. It is eerie because Sally NEVER sits still, especially when someone is on the floor at her level.

When the pet psychic opens her eyes, Sally lunges

back into her lap and licks her face.

"She just loves life," the psychic says, as she laughs and snuggles with Sally.

The psychic tells me the first thing she does when she connects with a pet is to ask permission to communicate. She says Sally's response to this question was, "you can talk?" followed by the mad licking of the face. The next response Sally made, according to the psychic, was she loved, loved, loved her mom (that would be me!). I am smiling like mad at this point, but I resist licking the psychic's face.

And what about Louis? The pet psychic asked Sally – through mental communication -- what was up with the cat.

"Sally says Louis is arrogant!" the psychic says.

Arrogant?

I watch Louis strut across the room, tail straight up in the air, and laugh. Yeah, he's arrogant.

"Sally likes Mary," the pet psychic states, "but she thinks Mary is a bump on a log."

"What?" I am confused. "Bump on a log? We have to give her a doggy sedative at night so she doesn't pace around our bed, her nails clicking on the hardwood floors."

The psychic shrugs.

"Mary is a ball-chasing, bundle of nerves," I continue, then pause. "Of course, when it comes to playing with Sally, she really doesn't show much interest."

"Sally was also excited that you might learn how to talk to her," the psychic says.

I am all for it. Under the psychic's direction, I sit with my eyes closed and try to focus on Sally. I want to tune into Sally's psyche, but I can't zone out of the present.

I might try again, though, because I really want to know what's going on with the licking of my husband's face when we go to bed at night.

That's Sally licking his face, not me.

Life Without Mom

By Sally McDonald
Ghost written by Michael P. McDonald

When the suitcase came out, I had a sinking feeling in the pit of my stomach. I thought it was indigestion, but soon realized the unthinkable was occurring: Mom was leaving.

The details were unimportant, since I was overwhelmed by her selfishness. How dare she do something without taking my needs into consideration? My initial pangs of anger soon morphed into blind, maniacal panic. What would I do for three days without her? Who would let me in and out the moment I wanted it to happen? Who would respond to my whimpers and barks and be able to decipher my needs unerringly? Not Dad. He's a good guy, and he's adequate for basics, like food and shelter. But who are we kidding? He's not Mom!

As her car pulled out of the driveway, and the last sounds of the garage door closing dissipated, I was left with the reality of a very bad situation. Mary, my cocker-lab sister, did not seem too concerned, as she lay snoozing. I wasn't sure if that was a result of her maturity and wisdom or the remnants of her anti-anxiety medication.

Once Dad got home, things didn't get much bet-ter. He gave me the same food for dinner, but it just tasted better when Mom gave it to me. For her it was an act of love and worship, not just some perfunctory, menial act. Even after dinner when Dad was throwing my lacrosse ball for me, he kept throwing it after I was tired. Mom would know when the first pangs of fatigue were setting in and not push me. She knows I am much too delicate, despite my overly developed musculature, to be treated like it's the first week of football training camp.

The evening didn't help alleviate my sour mood. First, Dad paid attention to Mary and the cats while I was in the same room. I know Mom is nice to the other guys once in awhile, but at least she has the common decency to do it outside of my presence. It's like he was throwing it in my face.

Then as Dad sat reading, why didn't he sit in the right chair? Even when he invited me on his lap, why weren't his legs in the proper alignment to facilitate my comfort and favorite position? Just as I was getting comfortable, he had to get up and go to the bathroom. I sure missed Mom's large bladder capacity.

Bedtime was when the real nightmare began. First, we got into bed an hour later than I'm used to. And once the lights went off, things went from bad to worse. Dad had no idea how to position his legs to create the *cave* Mom makes for me every night. He had the nerve to use his entire pillow for his head. What if I wanted to put my head up there? This was going to be a long night.

The next two days didn't get much better. Why didn't he know that every time he went into the kitchen he was supposed to give me a doggy bone? Did he think I was following him in there doing my little happy whirling dervish spinning routine for my health? My God man, you're killing me!

I thought things were going to get better when Dad went outside to do yard work. When he got out the hose to water the plants, I figured it was playtime, like Mom and me do for hours at a time. He let me jump at the spray for a couple minutes. He even shot it right into my mouth. I was having a great time. But then as soon as it began, it was over. How does he not have the ability to read my mind and play with the water for as long as I am still interested?

That night I was playing it a little standoffish. I wouldn't go to Dad when he asked me to sit with him. I wouldn't chase my ball when he wanted me to. I was going to show him who was boss and get things back on track. Then the pizza arrived. Mom never, ever lets me eat people-food, but Dad enticed me with pizza crusts.

The next morning came quickly, either because I had to get outside early due to last night's pizza gorge-fest or due to my excitement that Mom was coming home.

When I heard the sound of her car in the distance, I began spinning in crazy, exhilarated circles. By the time she pulled into the driveway I was so dizzy I could barely stand, but there she was. She squatted down, and I blasted into her. I lost track of how many kisses I gave her.

It felt like she had been gone forever and like she had never left, all at the same time. My world was right again!

Dead Things Can Be Bad For You

"It's right there by your left foot," I say.

A fresh mound of greenish-colored Sally feces nestles among the red and orange leaves of a Michigan fall.

"Give me the Ziploc," Mike says. He takes the bag, turns it inside out and scoops the mess into it. Turning the bag right side out, Mike seals it and heads toward the garage. I follow behind, my hand over my mouth.

"What is all this stuff?" Mike examines the bag. "It looks like fur or hair."

I make a perfunctory look at the bag of disgusting substance and hurry to the bathroom where I wash my hands up to my elbows. I haven't even touched anything, but still need to scrub.

It started two days earlier, Sunday, when we spent the day outdoors. Mike worked on blowing the leaves into the woods and I planted flower bulbs. Mary chased her ball, and Sally was a pest. She stole my bulb planter and chewed on the wooden handle. She dragged the shovel into the middle of the yard where Mike was blowing the leaves. She took Mary's tennis ball from her. Not to chase it, mind you, just to get Mary's attention.

Later that night Sally didn't have much pep. I blamed her lethargy on overdoing an outside day in the cool fall air. Little did I know the real reason.

Two days later, Sally still isn't feeling well. When I walk past our bed, she is curled asleep with her long nose tucked under her paws. Normally she will open her eyes when she hears me walk in, but this time she doesn't.

"Sally?"

No response.

"Sally!" I pat her side and still no reaction. I am close to panic when she opens her eyes and peeks at me. But there is no tail wagging.

"Mike, something's wrong with Sal."

My husband comes into the room and scoops Sally into his arms. He sets her on the floor. She falls back onto her haunches, with no energy.

My eyes fill with tears. "Mike, we have to do something."

I call my sister, Kendra, who has worked with veterinarians for years.

"Something is wrong with Sally," I say. Kendra is used to my near-panic calls when one of our pets is ill or hurt and the vet's office is closed.

"What's going on?" she asks in her calm voice, meant to reassure me that everything is going to be okay.

I give her the whole rundown, ending with the greenish fur stuff. "It sounds like she ate something she shouldn't have and now has a stomach ache."

Why hadn't I thought of that?

That night, Sally and I sit in bed together. I work on a crossword puzzle and she lays next to me. A smell seems to be emanating from both ends of her. It is as if something rotten, dead and horribly disgusting is living inside my little dog. It has the makings of a Stephen King novel. My stomach does flip-flops and dry-heaves.

The next day I take Sally to our vet and hand her the bag that is now double zip locked. Without any squeamishness, she begins feeling the feces through the bag.

"Where did all this black fur come from?" she asks. She continues squeezing the bag. "Uh oh, I think this is a little paw."

"You're kidding," I say, my stomach lurching.

"What have you been eating, Sally?" The vet laughs and at that point, an odor emanates throughout the room. She opens the window.

After a thorough examination, she determines that Sally is running a temperature and surmises Sally has indeed eaten something not only dead, but rotten. She now has a gastrointestinal infection. I guess the some-thing might have been one of the squirrels we are always chasing out of our bird feeders.

After a couple of shots and three different medica-tions, Sally and I are back in the car on our way home.

"Sally," I say. She lifts her head off the seat and looks at me. "From now on, when you find something disgusting, please don't eat it. Just roll in it."

I will live to regret those words.

The "Arf" of Painting

Sally is going to a doggie painting class. And yes, there is such a thing.

Arfs & Crafts is offered by Carol Bordua at Pawsitive Training by Dunewood in Grand Haven. The class will meet for one-hour sessions for three weeks. Sally can paint on ceramics, glass or canvas. Knowing Sally's penchant for whirling dervishness, I choose the only thing unbreakable, canvas.

My first goal is to get Sally to raise her paw. This is easy, thanks to Jake, who has taught Sally to shake. Sally knows four commands: spin, sit, down and shake. The problem is she doesn't see these as separate entities and will do them in succession as one continuous trick.

Knowing how to shake means Sally knows how to raise her paw. Sally will sit, stare intently at a treat and lift her paw. I reinforce this move with a click and then yummy treats. With Sally's love of food, this is a very effective incentive!

Next we give the stroke a name. I choose the word paw, and "Sally, paw!" "Sally, paw!" "Sally, paw!" becomes my mantra. Each time she strokes her paw, tasty kitty treats follow. We are out of doggie treats and I have improvised. Doggie treats, kitty treats, what's the difference, right? I would soon discover that difference.

We then introduce a mock painting pad (a plastic clipboard), which proves to be the undoing for the night.

"Sally, sit. Sally, paw." Click! Treat, perfect. I hold out the clipboard, "Sally, paw" and she backs away. Why? Who knows what goes on in that rock-like head of hers?

At home that night, Sally is snoring in bed beside me, and I am chuckling about our first class. Then I hear that familiar dog's-going-to-throw-up noise. Apparently excessive amounts of kitty treats are not a good idea. While changing the bed sheets I decide a trip to the pet store for doggy treats the next day is a necessity.

We practice at home that week with a plain piece of cardboard without much success. That non-success continues during the next class. On the occasions when Sally's paw does accidentally hit the cardboard, I praise and reward her with an array of delicious doggie treats. She bores of that activity.

We move on to placing the Paintin' Paw on her foot. I expect her to sit and hold her paw up, or limp with it on, but she wears it like a pro and I am encouraged. The Paintin' Paw slips over the foot and is fastened with Velcro. During the process, a sponge is dipped in the paint and then attached to the underside of the Paintin' Paw. In a perfect world, with the paint on the pad and the command "paw," Sally will stroke the canvas and ta da – a painting. I can only hope.

The ride home from class is quiet, with Sally snoozing on the seat beside me. She waits until we get out of the car before she throws up the doggie treats.

Sally's artistic debut arrives and Mike accompanies us to the big event. A large blue tarp is spread on the floor to contain excessive paint, and I put Sally's Paintin' Paw on her with great anticipation. Mike dips a sponge in blue paint; I attach it, and hold out the canvas.

Sally looks away. Sally yawns. Sally rolls on the plastic tarp. Sally stands on my leg with blue paint oozing through my pants. She shows no interest in pawing, stroking or getting paint on the canvas in any way.

She is interested in what the other dogs are doing, and she is interested in where Carol is standing. She is even interested in the treats, as long as she doesn't have to lift her paw to get them.

I beg, I plead. I am stern. She is not interested. I look at Mike who laughs and shrugs his shoulders. Sally chases her tail.

We change sponge colors, and soon Sally is slipping on the paint-streaked tarp. Her butt is blue from sitting in paint, and she has a red steak down her nose, but there is little paint on the canvas.

"Sally, paw!" She tugs the pad off her paw. I sit in desperation and Sally climbs into my lap. We look around at the other dogs. The Rhodesian ridgeback is using both paws to paint so his owners have to switch the Paintin' Paw. The chocolate lab is using a variety of colors, and the collie is painting a whole set of pottery. Is that pity I see on their owners' faces when they look at Sally?

Sally is getting more paint on me than she is on her canvas. We should frame my jeans.

On the drive home, I hold up the canvas. "What do you think?" I ask my husband.

He gives it a quick glance, and Sally belches.

"I think Picasso can rest easy," he says.

Sibling Rivalry

"How cute is this?" I say, holding up a green sweater with red trim. Nicole is home from college on Christmas break and we are spending the day shopping at the mall. "Wouldn't Sally look adorable in this?"

Nicole shakes her head and rolls her eyes at me. She has always been a little touchy about my Sally obsession, feeling somehow like Sally has taken her place as the *favorite daughter*. I've told her she was being too sensitive, but I have to admit that sometimes the line gets a little blurry between my human daughter and my dog daughter.

"Mom, since when did you become one of those people who dress their dog?" Nicole says.

"I'm not. But, you know, Sally does get cold outside in the snow."

Nicole grabs the sweater from my hand and looks it over. "Yeah, yeah, it would look cute on the little brat."

When we make our way to the checkout lane, I take the two pair of jeans from Nicole's arms and put them with the Sally sweater. "My treat," I say, a feeble attempt at trying to restore sibling harmony.

Later we decide it is a great day to take both dogs for a walk down by Lake Michigan. I go out to start the car and wait for Nicole. When she walks into the garage, she stops short.

"Why is Sally in the front seat?" she asks. "You don't expect me to sit in back, do you?"

"Sally loves the heated seat, and with her short fur you know how easily she gets cold." As soon as the words are out of my mouth, I realize the mistake I have made. "I'm just kidding," I say, forcing a chuckle. "Sally, backseat!" I scoot Sally onto a fluffy blanket in the backseat with Mary. The ride to the lake is an awkward silence, and my sense is Nicole was not fooled.

That night, Nicole and I snuggle down on the couch to watch a movie together, one of our favorite things to do when she visits. The movie is funny, the popcorn the perfect blend of butter and salt, and life is good, until Sally starts forcing her way onto the couch between us. When we don't let her up, she sits back on her haunches and lets out a sharp bark that is directed at Nicole. Ignoring her is not an option, so we let her up and she sprawls across my lap. She stretches out and little by little nudges Nicole to the end of the couch.

When the movie ends, Nicole looks at me. "Mom? Will you get up and change the movie?"

A perfect question since this is the normal protocol in our movie watching, as I usually have to take a bathroom break between movies.

The problem is I can't move because Sally is sleeping on my lap. She looks so cute with her little white rock-like head resting on my leg, snoring. My trance-like observation of Sally is interrupted by Nicole's voice.

"You're not getting up because that dog is in your lap?"

Let's just say our mother-daughter togetherness takes an ugly turn at this point.

Later that night we go through our normal nighttime routine. Sally lays on the bed. Sally chews her bone. Sally licks Mike's face. Sally burrows under the covers and falls sleep. Nicole is on the couch watching TV since she is still operating in the college vampire time-zone.

In the morning Sally is not in bed with us, which is odd because she loves her sack time. Mary is still asleep in her bed, but no Sally. I check in the bathroom by the heater vent, another favorite Sally morning spot, but still, no Sally.

Pushing the door open a bit, I peek into Nicole's room. On the pillow next to Nicole's head, I see a little white snout. There is Sally with Nicole's arm draped across her.

It appears Nicole has finally embraced "Sally love." Maybe now I can stop feeling guilty.

Snowbound Sally

"Sally!"

She skids to a stop in the snow, turns and bounds toward us. Mike and I are taking the dogs for a walk to the mailbox and everywhere we look is a winter wonderland. The cold crunches under our boots, and the woods surrounding us are filled with trees heavy-laden with snow, their boughs bending toward the ground.

The road has been plowed by our neighbor, and the banks lining it are several feet high, with the snow beyond them a foot deep of fluffiness.

Mary and Sally run ahead of us down the road, zigzagging back and forth from one snow bank to the other. Their heads are close to the ground as they sniff every indentation along the way. Mary's reddish fur stands out like a beacon, and white Sally is wearing her green sweatshirt to make it easier to spot her in the whiteness of this winter wonderland. She leaps onto a bank, dives into the snow on the other side, and pops up covered with the wintry powder. She hops through the deepness like a bunny, then turns and jumps back onto the road.

Mike throws a neon tennis ball down the road, and Mary takes off like a greyhound on a racetrack. She is obsessed with chasing her ball, and the weather doesn't alter this behavior in the least. She spots it in a bank and stops, as graceful Sally slides into the back of her, and they both fall into each other. Mary leaps up, grabs the ball and races back to us, dropping it at our feet. Sally's paws are moving in different directions as she struggles to get up. Distracted by a branch, she stops to play tug of war.

It is snowing big fluffy flakes, and I try to catch one on my tongue. The snow globe we have been walking in has been shaken.

Up ahead we see Mary drop to the ground and start rolling. "She is so cute," I say to Mike. When we look closer, we realize she has found a dog-tantalizing pile of horse manure.

"Mary!" She pauses as she looks at us, then jumps up and dashes down the path. Sally runs by the dog appealing aroma without so much as a glance, chasing after Mary. Her naiveté is so appreciated at this point.

At the mailboxes we tell them to sit while I get the mail. They tremble with the anticipation of once again running through the snow. When we turn back towards the house, a simple "Okay" is all it takes for them to take off, snow raising like dust under their paws.

They run ahead, Mary with her ball in her mouth, and Sally struggling to keep up with Mary's speed. Sally edges Mary toward a snow bank, trying to push her off the road, when Mary drops and cuts in behind Sally. Mary deftly avoids the snow bank Sally runs into. Like a pinball in a machine, Sally bounces off the bank and back

onto the plowed road. She stops, chases her tail, climbs over another snow bank and is soon hopping among the trees. She finds the trail of something, a rabbit or maybe a deer, and buries her long bull terrier nose deep into the tracks. We call her name, and she bounds toward us, face covered in snow. She does a full-body shake that begins with her head and ends with her tail.

We continue our walk, hand in hand, laughing at Sally's antics and stopping to pick up Mary's ball and throw it for her. It has been several weeks of snow, blizzards and more snow. For Michigan this is normal winter behavior, but I have felt housebound, and this walk has helped energize my lungs with cool, fresh air.

Watching Sally hopping through the deep snow, burying her face into the paw print of some other animal, and then running full tilt down the road toward us has lifted my soul and brought laughter to my lips. I am looking at this snow filled world with a fresh eye.

At the back door we stomp the snow off our boots, and I reach down to take off Sally's snow-covered sweatshirt. She gives me an affectionate nibble on my earlobe and I laugh out loud.

Life with Sally ... good in all kinds of weather.

Hotel Sally

Aaahh … spring break! Exotic locations, tropical sun and warm weather for many, but for Sally, spring break is the arrival of Sophie, a three-year-old black Schnoodle.

Like a movie star, Sophie's entourage carries her into Hotel Sally, then totes in her kennel with fluffy pad, food, treats, favorite chew bone and leash. There is a big fanfare of kisses and hugs from her human family, and they are out the door.

Sophie scratches at the glass entrance as her family backs out of the driveway. I scoop her up. This curbs the yapping that has been emanating from her since they walked out. It is a high pitched, curl-the-hair-on-the-back-of-your neck kind of yapping and I look at the windows to see if they are cracking.

I set her down, and there is the obligatory dog-sniffing. Sally starts her maniacal spinning, her OCD way of expressing happiness. Sophie appears spellbound until

Sally spins into her, knocking her down. This is met with a lip-curling sneer.

Sophie is a cross between a poodle and a schnauzer. She is the ebony to Sally's ivory.

We take the dogs for a walk, and Sophie stays close to us, while Sally runs ahead. She comes back to nudge Sophie into a game of tag but to no avail as Sophie remains our shadow.

That night, everyone settles down into our Sophie bedtime routine. It is different than our normal habit in that Mike and Sophie sleep in the guest room, while Sally and I sleep in our bed. How did this come about?

Sally sleeps in our bed at night. Right or wrong, she does. She has since the middle of her first night when, exhausted from her continuous crying, I put her in bed with us. She snuggled under the covers and a tradition was born.

Sophie sleeps in a bed at night. We didn't ask why or with whom, we just understood that is where she sleeps. And when she is at Hotel Sally, she sleeps with us, or rather, with Mike.

During Sophie's previous stay, we went to bed with Sally under the covers and Sophie asleep on the pillows. All was peaceful and quiet, until the middle of the night when Sally crawled out from under the covers. Sophie started growling. A dog growling on the pillows beside your head is not how you want to wake up.

We put Sophie in her kennel, where she cried for the rest of the night. The idea to sleep in separate beds was hatched somewhere in those sleep-deprived, dog crying, wee hours of the morning.

It doesn't take long for Sophie to settle into our schedule, and during the day, while I sit in my office and write, she joins the other furry creatures in the household and lies on the floor near my desk. I have to be careful when I move my chair, lest I roll onto a critter lying between my feet.

When we leave the house, Sophie is put into her kennel, and when we return, she greets us with more of the ear-splitting yapping. It is a race to release her from the kennel and us from the noise.

We take our walks, and soon Sophie is venturing away from the two-foot radius around us to run and play with Sally in the snow banks.

In the evenings, she and Sally vie for the spot on my lap that appears to be the most comfortable location in the entire house. At the beginning of the week, it is obvious by the sneering and lip-curling that my lap is

only big enough for one dog at a time. But after a few days, it has morphed into a spot where Sophie and Sally can lie together. At least until my legs start falling asleep.

The days tick by and soon it is time for Sophie to go back to her family. Spring break is over. When we walk into the house later that day, there is no urgency to quiet the yapping. But there is also no adorable little black dog expressing the unconditional joy of seeing us simply walk through the door.

That night, Sally sprawls across my lap as I watch TV, and later, Mike and I crawl into the same bed. The ghost of Sophie lingers under my desk chair, on my lap, and during our walks … until next year, when Hotel Sally will be happy to open its doors to her again.

The Endless Road Trip

Treats ... check! Water bowl ... check! Toys ... check!

Sally is going on a road trip.

We are visiting our friends in Niles, Michigan, and Sally is accompanying us on the road trip. As a puppy, she was a great passenger, content to curl on someone's lap and spend the trip sleeping. However, the last few journeys have been a flurry of back-and-forth leaps between the front and back seats, tangling up with my son's head phones, and filling the car with a horrible smell emanating from her backside. Still, we're gluttons for punishment and try to put those past excursions out of our minds.

Queen Mary hates to go visiting. She trembles and hides behind our legs. She is much more content to stay in her familiar surroundings with her pillow and tennis balls. Jake has agreed to stay home with her.

Mike puts the backseat down and lays out a

blanket with Sally's pillow bed. We think this will keep her content in the backseat. We are so gullible. I pack a bag with Sally's stuff for the weekend, along with bribes like treats, treats and more treats, to help keep our sanity during the drive.

It is a cool, sunny morning in March when we back out of the garage. Mike is driving. I am in the passenger seat and Sally is, for the moment, lying on her pillow in the back. The rubber ball she loves is lying between her front paws.

Five minutes later she drops the ball, and it rolls under the fold-down seats. She pokes her snout down the opening, then sits back and barks. I jump. She barks again and again and again. In Sally language this translates to "Hey! Get my ball."

"What does she want?" my husband asks.

Sally is staring down between the seats. I reach behind with my right arm, but can't reach the ball. I reach behind with my left hand, and I can just barely touch it. I give it a little shove, and it rolls over to my right hand. I grab it and am reminded of a Pilates workout as my body twists around in a way no human body should. Sally jumps into my lap with a thud.

I give her the ball as she settles into my lap for more gnawing. Then she drops it on the floor between my feet. I lurch forward and the seatbelt jerks me back with a jolting grip. Sally slides headfirst between my legs, toward the floor. My seatbelt releases its choke-hold, and I reach for her while the ball slides under my seat.

"What is going on over there?" Mike says.

He laughs as I contort myself into a pretzel and

manage to pull the ball out from under my seat. I push Sally into the back.

"This is ridiculous," I mumble. My black sweater is covered with white fur. What was I thinking when I decided to wear black? Sally starts barking again. We have been in the car a total of 30 minutes. This does not bode well for our 90-minute drive.

I give Sally a treat, hoping to distract her from the ball she has dropped behind Mike. The distraction lasts for a moment, and then she wedges herself under the fold -down seats. She scootches forward, then backwards, then forward again. She is stuck. She stops moving and barks once, twice, and then tries turning to the side.

"What is she doing back there?" Mike asks as she bumps into the back of his seat while trying to turn around.

"Come here Sally," I say.

She starts the forward and backward movements again. I unhook my seatbelt and lean halfway between the seats, grabbing at her rear. Giving a little tug, she wiggles out of the trapped location, and I boost her onto the backseat. I hide her ball under the towel on my lap.

I try to manipulate her into good behavior with the treats, which only lasts for the second that it takes her to devour them. I put the windows in the back down an inch, and she spends the next 10 minutes running back and forth, putting her long snout up to the opening and sniffing. The windows are now covered with dog slobber.

I give her a Kong, a hard rubber dog toy. That keeps her distracted, and the next 30 minutes are drama-free. But the rest of the trip is a repetition of back seat to front seat to backseat to … you get the idea.

When we arrive at our destination, Sally bounds out of the car and into the house to play with Griffin, our friends' German shepherd.

I flop onto the couch, already dreading the drive home.

A Love Affair

Sally is in love … with our gas grill.

This grill is nothing fancy. No burner on the side, no special knobs, just a plain ole' grill. And every winter we put the cover on it and store it in our pole barn, where it often becomes a home for some wayward mouse. In the spring, we get it out and move the mouse nest and its occupants to a safe spot in the barn. Then we scrub and disinfect the grill and put it out on the deck where it stays until fall.

This year my son and nephew moved the outdoor furniture, including the grill, out of the barn. They checked for mice (and found none), but they didn't clean out the grill before they put it in its usual spot. No big deal as I will give it a thorough cleaning on one of these warm spring days. However, it appears that the smell of mouse is very enticing to a certain miniature bull terrier.

Sally and I spend a great deal of time outside soaking up the sun. I plant flats of marigolds and impatiens.

Sally and Mary follow me around the yard, dropping their toys in my lap or in the pot where I am planting flowers. This is their not-so-subtle way of getting me to throw the balls for them. And being the good doggie mom that I am, I oblige.

I am busy digging, weeding and throwing when I realize there is only one nose pushing the tennis ball toward my hand. And it isn't Sally's distinctive long, white snout. I look around, but I am not too concerned as we live in a wooded area away from busy streets, and Sally has never been a wanderer, except when she finds a disgusting dead thing in the woods to snack on or roll in. But I digress. I spot her stretched out on the deck and go back to my tasks at hand. Mary returns to encourage me to throw her ball, and the hours pass. I keep my eye on Sally as she continues to hang out on the deck, next to the grill. The fact that she is staying in one location, while awake, should be a clue that something is amiss.

I hear a whine. It isn't one of those "I'm hurt" whines, but rather the "I want something, so get it for me now" whines. Sally is scratching at the grill. I figure she has pushed her ball underneath and can't reach it, so like the over-attentive-Sally-owner I am, I immediately go to help her. When she sees me coming, she starts circling and barking at the grill. I move it around but find nothing underneath or behind it.

"Sally, there's nothing under there," I say. I back up and trip on Mary's ball.

Sally is now pushing the handle of the grill up and down, up and down. I decide it is time to go in the house.

Once inside, Sally stands at the sliding doors, staring outside and barking to be let out. When I open the door, she runs to the grill. She sticks her nose under the bottom of the grill as far as she can, or she scratches at the

deck where it stands, or she circles it. When I push it closer to the railing, she wedges her body behind it until she has access to its entirety. No doubt, she is obsessing.

"What happened to Sally's nose?" my husband asks when he gets home. She has rubbed her nose raw from pushing her snout under the grill.

"For some reason, Sally is fascinated with the grill," I say.

We open every compartment and even turn the grill upside down, just so Sally can see there are no mice in or around the contraption. We are doing something rational for an irrational dog. Of course, it doesn't work.

The next day I open the sliders to another sun-filled day, and Sally runs past me, flies off the deck in her superman-leap, and chases Mary to the edge of the woods. I am happy we are putting the gas grill obsession behind us. I should have known better.

The grill is now a babysitter of sorts, for me. While I am outside I don't have to worry about where Sally is, although I do shake my head every time I hear her whining or scratching at the bottom of it.

Mike and I are thinking of retiring this worn-out grill and getting a new one this year. But with Sally's new fixation, it looks like we'll have to take her with us when we go shopping.

Disappearing Act

It would appear Sally is a Houdini-dog.

Sally's mini bull terrier fur is very, very short and needs little grooming. However, she does need bathing and nail trimming. On the other hand, Mary, our cocker-lab mix, needs regular grooming or she turns into a matted mess. Plus, she has shown a fondness for our neighbor's compost pile, which means she comes back after an investigation of its contents reeking of foul odors. And although Sally has not discovered this mound of smells, she does manage to find disgusting items – usually dead and decomposing items -- in the woods behind our house. And in the way that dogs do, she insists on rolling in whatever she finds.

So every few months our mobile dog groomer, Ingrid David of Lucky Dog Pet Salon, pulls her fully equipped van into our driveway. Inside are all the things needed to groom, bathe and dry a dog.

Our usual routine is that Ingrid arrives at 8 in the

morning. Mary is our Nervous Nellie, so I carry her out to the van while she quivers in my arms. With age, her nervousness is increasing, which necessitates a nighttime canine sedative to help her (and us) sleep. Nothing will keep you awake like the click-click-click of dog nails on hardwood floors as the dog paces around your bed ALL night.

Sally and I wait in the house for Mary, and when she is done being trimmed, shampooed and fussed over, she scampers inside showing off her new "do." Then it's Sally's turn.

During a recent appointment, Ingrid shows up early because I have to leave for work. The plan is that I will carry Mary to the van, leave for work, and after Mary is done, Ingrid will take care of Sally.

What was I thinking?

I carry Mary to the van whispering in her ear that "everything is okay," as Sally prances around my feet. After getting Mary settled in the van and Sally settled back in the house, I leave. When I get home several hours later, both dogs meet me at the door.

Mary looks beautiful, with little blue bows on her ears. She is doing her usual auditory greeting, which is a nice way of saying she is barking incessantly and setting me up for future hearing aids. Sally comes flying up behind her, sliding and bashing into Mary's back end. I notice that Sally isn't wearing a neck scarf. Sally's fur is too short for bows, so she always gets a scarf.

I maneuver my way to the kitchen where I find a note from Ingrid. *I couldn't find Sally.* I am confused because Sally is running from bowl to bowl, gulping water in her normal obsessive compulsive disorder way.

There is a telephone message from Ingrid, also. "I hope you have Sally with you," she said. This is becoming quite a mystery, so I call her. She tells me she had checked all through the house three times and had even looked under the bed (I cringe thinking of all the dust bunnies huddled underneath). Sally was nowhere to be found. Ingrid had even rung the doorbell, but the only dog to respond was Mary. There was no indication that Sally could have gotten out of the house, and no one had been in or out while she groomed Mary. Ingrid assumed I had Sally with me.

Our house isn't that big. There is only one bedroom on the main floor, and Sally wasn't under the bed (remember the dust bunnies), and she doesn't fit under the couch. So where was she? The closet and basement doors were closed, and she doesn't, to my knowledge, know how to open the cupboards. And wherever she had been hiding while Ingrid searched for her, she had been quiet.

My guess, and mind you it is only a guess, is this: Sally has a fancy wicker dog kennel, and at a glance it is difficult to see if she is inside. There is also a huge fluffy pillow stuffed in the kennel, and she likes to burrow into the far corner of it, curling herself into a little ball. And since the kennel is tucked into a corner of our bedroom, it is easy to walk in and not even notice it. So, my guess is that she was snuggled into her pillow and wasn't coming out for anything.

Of course, the bigger dilemma following her disappearance is that Sally still needs a bath. This means washing her in our bathtub, which involves a great deal of acrobatics on my part.

"Sally, let's take a bath," I call as I start running the water.

But she has already worked her magic and disappeared.

A Bathing Saga

I bend into a pretzel while scrubbing Sally in our bathtub. There is more water on me than her. She stands rigid, muscles taut, and refuses to look at me. Sally hates getting a bath. Suffice it to say, bath time is not a fun Mr. Bubbles experience for either of us.

So when I hear that Harborfront Hospital for Animals in Spring Lake is hosting a dog wash, I am enthusiastic. In addition to the obvious benefits of not having to wash a reluctant dog with muscles any wrestler would envy, I need a column idea for my monthly "Life with Sally."

Mike drives. Sally performs her usual car ritual: her front seat to backseat to front seat acrobatics. Let me tell you, catching and holding a 28-pound dog on your lap in a moving car is no easy feat. Try doing this while wearing shorts. Every time Mike reaches over to pet Sally, she lunges toward him, which results in my pulling her back, resulting in more scratches on my poor legs. By the time we get to the dog wash, my legs are bruised and tattooed with claw marks. I am not happy.

The parking lot is empty, and the sign on the door announces that the outdoor dog wash has been rescheduled for the following day due to rainy weather. Grrr!

The next day is a repeat of the one before. As we head toward the car, Mike yells, "I'll drive."

"No way," I respond, and we both dash to the driver's side, knowing that the passenger's lap would be Sally's seat. Mike hip-checks me out of the way.

I grumble, open the back door and load Sally and her stuff inside. By the way, when did a car ride with a dog become akin to a trip with a toddler? I rearrange the car seats so she can get in the back and lie down, even though the probability of that scenario is nil. I pack towels, treats, doggie water bowl, bottle of water and leash. The only thing we don't do is entertain her by singing car songs or playing games like "I spy with my little eye." I mean that would just be crazy, right?

After three backseat to front seat to backseat trips, Mike turns to me and says, "What's the matter? You seem a little stressed."

"That's because I have a dog walking back and forth over my lap."

"Sally, sit down," he commands. She stands on my lap and grins.

"Gee Mike, that worked really well," I say through clenched teeth.

Sally climbs into the backseat and then turns toward the console between the front seats.

"Sally, sit down," Mike repeats.

She slides onto the backseat and sits. For the next few miles, Mike continues his mantra of "sit down" and "stay." She sighs, and I glance back at her. She is giving me The Look. You know, the one that says, "I can't believe you're not letting me have my own way." She heaves another sigh and emits a sharp little "yap."

"What the heck was that?" Mike asks.

"The Princess is not happy." I raise my hand to pat her head but think better of it. She might interpret the gesture as an invitation to jump on my lap. I cherish the skin on my thighs and want them to remain intact and unbloodied.

After several more minutes of sits, stays, sighs and yaps, we make it to our destination.

I collect Sally, my camera and a notepad. This arrangement has disaster written all over it, so I hand the leash to Mike.

Walking to the check-in tent, we are greeted with, "Is that Sally from the magazine?" I beam and Sally starts her happy spinning dance. She loves being a celebrity.

At the first washing station, she is lifted onto a table. Three sets of loving hands scrub her, rinse her, give her a conditioning treatment and rinse her again.

But the happy dance has ended. Sally trembles throughout the entire process. Not a little quivering, mind you, but a full body get-me-out-of-here shaking. I massage her nose, Mike plays photographer, and the Sally washers give her lovin' the whole time. But the only time my girl quits trembling is when they offer her a spoonful of cheese from a can. Sally loves cheese!

After the scrubbing she is carried to the next station where she is rubbed dry with big fluffy towels. A bandanna is wrestled around her neck, and she is offered a bone the size of a small car. But Sally ignores it as she has only one thing in mind, a full body dry-off shake that

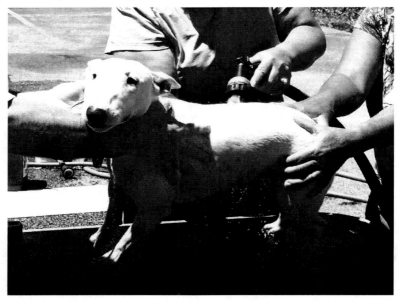

starts at her pointed little nose and ends at the very tip of her skinny white tail

I look back at the line and see a saint Bernard sharing the first washing station with a shar pei, and a golden retriever is off to the side, waiting for his turn. The song, *Car Wash*, is blasting from a CD player while people mingle with laughter. The sun's warmth spreads through my body, and it is my turn to sigh.

But Sally, who has finally abandoned her trembling, trots across the parking lot, her eyes riveted on a mud puddle.

Where Is Mary?

Mary is barking at the back door, but her barking sounds stifled. Not a painful yap. I know what that sounds like due to an unfortunate stepping-on-the-tail incident. No, this is two or three muted woofs, not unlike the muffled cat meow when Fluffy brings you a gift of a dead mouse.

My first thought: Did Mary have a dead rodent in her mouth? My second thought: Ick! I hope she hasn't eaten it.

I run down the stairs from my office. Sally runs ahead of me, stops to look back, runs again, and then stops again. I know Mary is in the backyard so I rush outside. Sally Superman leaps off the deck, lands in the grass and stops, swiveling her head from side to side. Mary's barking ceases. I call her name, no response. Sally runs to the patio deck and continues to look from side to side. I walk around the yard, calling Mary's name. Still, no barking.

Sally starts digging next to the patio.

"Sally, stop!" I command. A light bulb goes off. I run to the spot where Sally is digging, get down on my hands and knees in the grass, push aside the hostas and peer into the darkness. There is movement, and I am hoping it is Mary-movement, not some giant-rodent-movement. If there is a 30-pound rodent under my deck, Mary is on her own.

I hear a whimper, and yes, it is Mary. She is stuck in the one-foot space between the dirt and the patio deck. Then I hear a humming noise and am surrounded by a growing swarm of bloodthirsty mosquitoes. Slapping myself about the head, I make a mad dash to the house where I find I am covered with itchy welts.

How to get Mary out of there? I call my husband at his office for suggestions. He answers with a stern Mike voice that says, I can't talk now.

"Can you talk?" I ask.

"Not really."

I scratch at a rising welt. *Is this an emergency?* I thought. *No, I can handle this.* "I'll talk to you later," I say and hang up.

Grabbing a flashlight and towels, I head back to the deck. Kneeling on the towel, I shine the light under the deck. There she is, right dab in the middle of the 12 x 12 patio. "Come here, Mary." She wiggles and turns toward me, but she makes no progress. I am prepared to tear the patio apart board-by-board in order to free her. Mosquitoes buzz in my ears.

I will rake a path for Mary to crawl to freedom. I run to the garage and grab the rake. Sally follows me, spinning in her happy dance. Anything with a long handle is a toy to Sally.

I shine the flashlight under the deck. Hey! There is Sally's missing ball. I throw it across the yard. Sally runs after it, providing me with a slight reprieve from her garden tool obsession. I rake a swath from the middle of the patio deck to the edge.

"Come on, Mary." She wiggles backwards, then stops. I repeat the action from the other side of the deck. Same result.

Sally is back and wiggles between the deck and my face, kicks up soil and grabs at the rake. I spit out dirt.

"Sally, move." I nudge her with my elbow. She runs around me and grabs the rake from the other side, pulling it out of my hands. I swat mosquitoes. This is SO not working!

I hurry back to the garage and grab the can of bug spray. Empty! As I search through cupboards for a full can, I glance out the window. Sally is playing with a stick in the yard. *Wait a minute! That's the rake!* I head toward the door, and there is Mary!

"Mary," I say. "How did you get out of there?" I kneel down and run my hands over her body, checking for sore spots. She walks to her food dish and starts eating as if nothing has happened. I flop down on a chair and sigh with relief.

"All's well that ends well, eh Mary?" I say.

Sally runs by, dragging the rake.

"Toadal" Obsession

"Sally, drop that," my nephew Michel yells.

I am kneeling in a garden, pulling weeds but jump to my feet and hurry to the garage when I hear the tone of his voice. He stands over Sally, who is looking up at him.

"Drop it!" he says. She spits a brownish blob onto the cement.

"Ewww," I say.

Michel and I bend over to get a better look.

Sally will eat just about everything, except onions. And through our four years with our little white dog we have come to learn that although the item of Sally's desire may be dead, decaying and just plain grotesque, she will find it appealing. In fact, the level of Sally's interest in an object is proportional to its disgust-to-humans quotient. After all, there had been a recent dead squirrel episode that resulted in a stomach infection and a trip to the vet. I lean in for a better look, prepared to be grossed out.

"What is it?" Michel asks. I notice he keeps his distance.

This blob is the size of a large grape and puffy, with four little feet ... *webbed* feet. Toad feet. It is lying upside down in my driveway where it landed when Sally spat it out. I nudge it with my toe. It doesn't move. One thing is sure, the poor little toad is traumatized from its reluctant ride in a bull terrier's mouth.

I pick it up and turn it over in the palm of my hand. There is no blood, and it is breathing. Those are good signs. Meanwhile, Sally is spinning in her psychotic little happy dance and jumping at my hands.

"She's nuts," Michel says as he walks back to the wheelbarrow, shaking his head.

"What's your point?" I call to his back.

I put the distressed toad under a bench where Sally's stocky white body cannot reach it and go back to my gardening. For the next half hour Sally stares at the bench, barely moving a muscle, except for an occasional twitch of her black nose.

We have a lot of toads this year. Big toads and little toads; they seem to be everywhere. This has presented a new obsession for Sally ... toad chasing. This is the first instance where I saw her put one in her mouth, though. I shake my head in disgust.

Normally, she is in the yard with me while I'm gardening, and it's not unusual for her long white snout to be buried in the grass. Her head will jerk up as a toad, or whatever she's obsessing over, starts to flee. She follows it, her head bobbing up and down.

Following her nose, Sally has learned where

several large toads are camping out this summer. Every time she's in the yard she runs to these locations and sniffs like an addict. Sally will run from behind the garden hose spout, to the potted geranium on the front porch, and then behind the returnable container in the garage. The toads are smart enough to wiggle into an area where she is unable to reach them. So she will stand in front of their camps and whine.

On a few occasions, Sally has reached them before they can escape to their safe spot. Then, and this is the gross part, Sally will lick them. Seriously! *She licks them.* Just one lick and then she backs up and does the *blecch* thing with her tongue, not unlike a kid who's just sampled spinach for the first time. Then she'll run to the next spot, and if she finds a toad, *she will lick him* and repeat the backing-up, shaking-her-head routine. You would think she would learn. But then again, this is Sally.

After a day spent outside, Sally is moping around and giving me those *I'm sick* eyes. She won't jump on the bed, and she doesn't want to play with her ball. She isn't feeling well. I baby her all night, and when she still isn't acting any better the next day, I take her to the vet.

"She's been licking toads," I say. He laughs. His staff laughs. "No, I'm serious." They continue laughing.

After a thorough examination, the vet says she has a pinched nerve in her neck. I thought she had a toad digestion problem. Obviously her condition doesn't have anything to do with toad licking, so my diagnosis is way off.

"You know how sometimes you sleep wrong and wake up with a sore neck?" the vet says. "That's what she has."

I think back over the past couple days, trying to remember when this nerve pinching may have occurred. Then I remember the shovel. I had spent several hours planting a new perennial garden, and when I was done with the shovel, I tossed it in the grass. Sally stood staring at the shovel ... for about an hour.

"She does have an obsession with the shovel," I say to the vet.

He laughs. His staff laughs.

"No, I'm serious."

They continue laughing.

Camera Shy

A picture may tell a thousand words, but what happens behind the scenes is the real story. When it comes to taking photographs of Sally, a LOT goes on behind the scenes.

Sally is not camera friendly — once a camera comes out, she turns into Miss Shy Girl. Her pointed ears drop and she sneaks off to her kennel. Or she turns her back to the person holding the camera. So attempting to get photographs to go with the stories I write about my girl for the "Life with Sally" column is often an experience. In fact, it's an experience worthy of an entire column.

Several months ago, I spotted Sally barking and staring at herself in our metal trash container. I'd recently written a column about her fixation with the trash can and needed a photo.

I call Jake, and he comes over with his camera. I drag the garbage can out of the bathroom and into the hallway for better lighting. Plus, I don't think a photo of Sally, the container and the toilet will be all that interesting.

Sally sniffs at the trash can until Jake starts snapping photos. You would think he is the paparazzo the way she keeps avoiding him.

"Sally, here," I say and pat the container. She backs away. But our cat, Socks, wanders over, drops in front of the can and rolls around on his back. He is not camera shy. I scootch him out of the frame.

"Sally, look," I point to the can again. She backs away farther. Socks, the Camera Hog, wanders over again and rubs against the container. Jake keeps his eye in the viewfinder, ready for the shot. He taps his foot.

I get some cheese out of the refrigerator.

"Sally, want some cheese?" Sally loves cheese and starts her happy spinning. I lean over the container, trying to keep my legs out of the photo. Sally bounds toward me. Jake snaps pictures. Sally, her head cocked, backs away. I throw pieces of cheese at the container.

"Sally, get it," I say, pointing at the cheese. No forward movement.

I go back to the refrigerator. I need bigger treat ammunition and rummage for tuna fish. Socks comes running. I lock him in the basement.

I throw tuna at the container and it lands in front of the basement door. Sally ignores it. A gray cat paw shoots out from under the door and swipes at it.

"This is ridiculous," Jake says.

I make a path of tuna fish from Sally to the container. She eats the first couple of pieces, looks over her shoulder at the camera, and backs away.

I wrap tuna in cheese and throw it at the container. A piece sticks to the side. Sally sneaks forward, sticks her pink tongue out as far as possible, and Jake clicks the camera.

We have the shot!

Now I need a photo of Sally looking out the front window. Easy shot since she loves to stand at the window and look outside. I have a plan: I will go outside and crouch underneath the window and call Sally. She will stand up against the windowsill, and Jake can snap the photo. What can go wrong?

Yeah, right.

Sally refuses to come near the window as I call her from outside. Cheese comes to the rescue again, as we stick a piece of it on the windowsill. Sally's reluctance to get her picture taken will surely result in weight gain. I picture myself trying to explain that to the vet.

I put her in the bathtub for a bath shot. She sits with her back to Jake's camera and stares at the faucets. I turn her around and she whines as if I were attempting to drown her. There isn't even any water in the tub!

When she wasn't feeling well (after a dead squirrel incident), I took photos of her lying on the bed. She looked ill before the camera came out, but she looked like she was dying once the camera came in view.

On the other hand, candid shots can be amazing. The photos of her staring at a toad in the flowerpot, obsessing over the rake, and fixating on the grill were easy to get.

Staring, fixating and obsessing? Is there a theme

here?

Maybe I'm doing this backwards. Should I look at the photo and then write the story? If so, then this photo speaks of pure dog joy. Running through a field with long, green grasses tickling her pink belly. Running, jumping, leaping and happy.

Sally ... totally unaware of the camera clicking away.

The Beast

I am in the bathroom when I notice Sally isn't in her usual place. She loves to lay in front of the cabinets with her long, white snout wedged underneath, the heat from the register flowing over her big black nose. Now she is standing by the toilet, staring at something in the corner.

"Sally, what are you doing?" I don't know why I ask these questions – she never answers me. She is bobbing her head up and down, then leaning forward and then stepping back. I look at the object of her attention. It is our stainless steel garbage container and she can see herself in the reflection.

"You are a nut!" I say, relieved she didn't find a toad in the house. I scratch her butt. She wags her tail and turns back to her reflection, giving a little growl.

We spend the rest of the day outside. Mike mows the lawn, I pull weeds in the gardens, Mary chases her tennis ball, and Sally scours the pole barn searching for mice or toads.

Mary starts barking. I walk to the front of the house expecting to have a visitor, but no one is there. I spot her standing just inside the woods where she is barking with purpose, but from where I stand I can't see what it is.

"What is she barking at?" Mike calls from inside the house. He has gone inside to grab a glass of water.

I call her name, and she turns to look at me, then turns back.

I walk to the edge of the woods and look in the direction of her barking, seeing only logs and piles of dead leaves. Mary's tail is wagging wildly, so I know I am headed in the right direction. I'm just not sure what I am going to find. I tromp around some small trees, push aside branches and then I see it. A woodchuck, or maybe a groundhog. Someone later told me they were the same thing, but I don't know that at the time.

What I do know is this creature is standing up on its hind legs staring at Mary. I think of the comical golf course woodchuck in the movie, *Caddy Shack*, but then I remember that rodents have sharp little teeth. Would this one tear Mary apart in a wild battle? I hear myself gulp.

I take a step back, but continue staring at the little monster. "Mary, get over here!" She looks at me, but she doesn't move. "Mary, here!" I call again, panic in my voice as I imagine the horrible fight that is about to ensue. Mary inches toward me as I back through the trees.

"Mike!" I yell loud enough to be heard in the next county. "Mike, come here!" There is no movement from the house.

Mary has stopped barking and trots out of the woods. I keep my eye on the beast, which hasn't moved. From around the corner of the garage, a white blur streaks straight toward the woods where the giant rodent awaits.

"Sally, no!" I lunge and grab her by the back legs. All I can visualize is the woodchuck's sharp teeth. I struggle to hold Sally in my arms. She wiggles, bucks and squirms as I try to keep her rock-like head from connecting with my chin. I scoop her up and run across the lawn while screaming for Mary to follow.

Mike ambles out on the deck. "What's up?" he says, looking from me to Mary to Sally. We are all panting.

I put Sally down and Mary sits next to her on the deck, her tennis ball in her mouth.

"Mary found a woodchuck or a ground hog or something in the woods."

"Is it still there?"

"I'll check." I head back to the woods, while Mike keeps the dogs with him. The furry beast is still there, sitting in the exact same position. It doesn't look like he has moved an inch. "Mike, he's still here. Come see."

Mike puts the dogs in the house and trots over.

"I don't see anything."

"Right there," I point.

"I'm going to see how close I can get."

That phrase rings a bell in my head. Where had I heard it before? Oh yeah, in a horror movie, right before the unwitting victim gets attacked by some wild animal.

"Mike, I don't think that's such a good idea."

He ignores me and walks farther into the woods. The woodchuck/ground hog doesn't move. His whiskers don't move. His fur doesn't move. His head doesn't move. Nothing about him makes any movement.

Mike turns back to me. "Tricia, I think it's dead."

"He's not dead."

Mike moves closer. "No, he's dead."

"Mike, corpses don't stand on their hind legs." I stifle a laugh.

Mike takes another step closer to the dead groundhog. It turns and scurries deeper into the woods. Mike runs out of the woods, his eyes wide.

"I could see his little teeth," he says as he makes a phuffing sound.

"How was that again?" I ask. He repeats the noise.

We walk back into the house where Mary is pacing at the backdoor. Sally is nowhere in sight.

"Listen," Mike says. In the quiet, we can hear a faint growling noise. We follow the sound until we find Sally ... growling at her reflection in the garbage can.

Sally's New Year's Resolutions
A Mother's Wish List

1. Listen and obey Mom. I think this one is going to take some work … as in, a training course. Having taken a puppy class, Sally listens and behaves pretty well. But now everything is in "Sally-time," which is another way of saying when Sally wants to do something, she'll do it. Otherwise, forget about it.

2. Stop stalking Louis the cat. Now that Louis has moved to college with Nicole, this is one resolution that should be easy for Sally to accomplish. In fact, I'm sure she has already forgotten all about Louis.

3. Go for a walk or play outside at least once a day. Of course, this resolution is one that I, as her human mother, need to get on board with. I wonder if walking to the end of the driveway and back could be considered a walk. Sally and I chase each other up and down the stairs once in awhile. Is that exercise? Please say yes!

4. Stop being a wuss. I don't think Sally is a wuss, but it has been drawn to my attention that she isn't what you would call brave. For example, when she is outside and keeps looking over her shoulder, is that being a wuss or is that being *aware*? I'll go with aware.

5. Stop wearing ridiculous clothes. I still can't believe I'm dressing my dog. Who would have thought? But I take offense at the idea that they are ridiculous clothes. Well, maybe the shark costume was pushing the goofy look. But come on, a shark costume on Sally? Okay, that is ridiculous, so I'll put the shark costume away. It's time to get out the mint green quilted winter jacket and matching booties, anyway.

6. Learn how to ride in the car. I am right on board with this one. Jumping back and forth between the front and backseats is NOT appropriate. Standing on my lap is NOT appropriate, especially when I am wearing shorts and her claws are digging into my skin. Trying to climb on Mike's lap while he is driving — NOT appropriate. So in order to help Sally accomplish this resolution, I purchased a seat belt harness. We haven't used it yet, and I have no doubt that the first ride with this contraption is going to become a story in itself.

7. Overcome obsession with gardening tools. Rakes, shovels, hoes, brooms ... anything with a long wooden handle appears to be a toy to this little white dog. I don't get it. Digging a hole is almost impossible, and raking leaves ... not possible.

8. Overcome fear of garbage bags, things that go bump in the night, flushing toilets, and everything else in the world. What's up with the fear thing, anyway? Excuse me, perhaps she's just being *aware*.

9. Become a better guard dog. When I enter the house, I hear Sally barking from inside her kennel, in the corner of my bedroom, at the far end of the house. Mind you, the kennel is open. I'm not so sure this behavior is going to be intimidating to someone breaking into our home. In fact, I'm pretty sure we should leave guarding the house to Mary, whose ear-splitting barking would make a robber run screaming into the night.

10. Stop eating poop. Okay, it's a dog thing and I can't even comment. Ugh!

11. Don't roll in or eat disgusting, dead, foul-smelling things. Again, Ugh!

12. Overcome camera shyness. Ears down and slouching do not make for a good photo. Turning your back on cameraman Jake does not make for a good photo shoot. Just stand there and look pretty! Like that's ever going to happen.

13. Stop getting up in the middle of the night for a potty break. I'm all for this one. Although I love kisses from Sally, her licking my face at 3 a.m. has nothing to do with love and everything to do with having to go outside.

Early-morning bladder emptying is not conducive to a good night's sleep for anyone.

14. Work on social skills. We have a Christmas party every year, and our guests always ask, "Where is Sally?" And where is Sally? Sleeping in her kennel. As soon as the house clears, she's out and about looking for floor scraps. But until then, she's invisible.

15. Choose better places to pass gas. I think better places would be anywhere that isn't my lap. And phew! On a scale of 1 to 10, Sally's gas smell hits 11 or 12. So, let's just leave this one alone, too.

16. Continue being the loveable and unique Sally. This one will be easy.

A Romp In The Snow

"Oh, just look at these shoes," I gush to Nicole. We are doing a little Christmas shopping. The shoes are black faux leather with white straps around the ankle and a zipper up the front.

"Shoes?" Nicole has a package of squeaky mice in one hand and kitty treats in the other, stocking stuffers for the furry members of our family. She turns in a tight circle, looking up and down. "I don't see any shoes."

I reach past her and grab the plastic bag off the shelf. Inside are four doggy booties.

Her face scrunches into a mask of horror. "No, Mom. Absolutely not!"

"Look, they light up too." I take one of the booties out of the bag and bang it against the shelf. A red light blinks on and off at the toe of the boot. "Sally, would look …"

"Ridiculous." Nicole executes an eye roll.

"… adorable in these." I put my fingers inside two

of the booties and walk them along a shelf, watching the red lights blink in unison.

"Let me see those." Nicole drops the cat toys in our cart and takes the other pair of boots out of the bag. "What's happened to you?" she says, turning them over in her hands and looking at me. "You used to be so normal, and now you're looking at booties for Sally?" She knocks them against my arm, and the red lights start blinking. Her face softens. "They are pretty cute, though."

We throw them in our cart. A few hours later, while unpacking the groceries, I spot the forgotten booties.

"Nicole!" I say. "We have got to try these on Sally."

Putting our own coats, boots, and scarves back on, we walk outside with Sally close on our heels. Sitting on the steps, I hold her on my lap, and we slip each paw into the stunning boots. After zipping up the front and tightening the Velcro strap, I set Sally on the ground.

It's hard to put into words what happens next. Sally takes off running through the garage to the snow-covered driveway. Running, however, doesn't really describe her gait. It is like side-kicking. Each paw flicks out to the side, sometimes in unison and sometimes in a singular movement. And the red lights are blinking and blinking and blinking. I know; it's hard to visualize.

Nicole and I clutch each other and laugh. No, it is more than just laughing. It is hysteria. You know, the laughing where you're grasping your stomach and bending over? We fall into each other, holding on as we watch Sally continue her four-legged side-stepping

forward-run. My legs are weak from the laughter bub-
bling up inside of me.

Mary, our non-booted dog, slides to a stop in the
snow and watches as Sally runs up to her. She sniffs at
the boots, but then Sally starts spinning, legs flying in
different directions. One of the back booties flies off, and
lands in a snow bank. But that doesn't stop Sally. She
continues her side-running. The fluffy snow kicking up
behind her ... or maybe it is beside her. I am watching
through tear-filled eyes, so everything is a bit blurry.

"Stop!" Nicole says, bent over at the waist. "Make

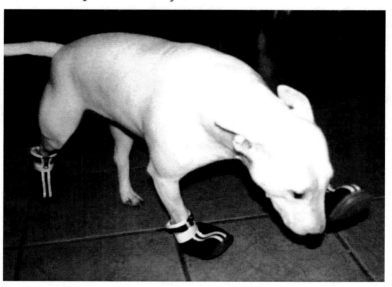

her stop, I can't stand it anymore."

Sally is standing at the end of the walkway,
watching us. She doesn't seem to be in any distress over
having to wear the boots, and isn't pulling or biting at
them. She just stands there with that silly grin, her dark
eyes sparkling with mischief.

"Come on Sally," I say. "Let's go in the house." She tears toward us, legs flailing, snow flying, and it starts again. The laughter, that is. I clutch at the stitch in my side.

Nicole and I wipe tears from our faces.

"That was the funniest thing I've ever seen," she admits.

"I know. I can't wait to show Mike." I pick up Sally and give her long white snout a big kiss while Nicole removes the other three boots.

We decide it would be funny to put the boots on Mary, but she won't come near us as long as we have them in our hands.

Several hours later Mike and Jake pull into the garage. Grabbing Sally, Nicole and I pop the boots back onto her paws.

"Hey guys, wait until you see this," Nicole says as we hurry outside.

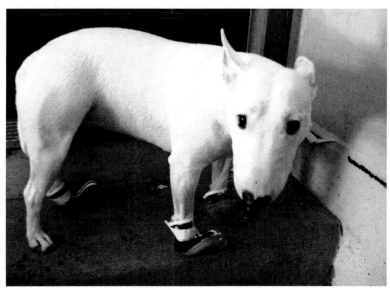

Purple Sally Holder

Sally's idea of a car ride is full access to every inch of the car during the entire ride. Translated: if she wants to be in the backseat, she's there. If she wants to be in the front seat, she's there. Passenger floor by my feet, there. Back on my lap, there. Face pressed against the window, yup, you got it ... there. This involves total Sally movement, all the time. Now imagine those old movies where the film is fast-forwarded and the characters are moving so fast, they're practically a blur. That's Sally on a car ride.

I know. I know. This means I am not a good dog trainer, and she walks all over me. Believe me. I've heard this repeated once or twice before. More often than not by my husband.

Now here we are, taking another car ride with her, and no one is looking forward to it, except Sally. Her tail is wagging as I open the back door. She jumps onto the seat, then wiggles her way through the bucket seats into the front.

"Sally, come back here," I say.

Listen, I love my dog. I mean I loooove my dog. But stress I can do without, and my neck muscles are already getting tight. Sally dives back through the seats and slams her 25 pound muscled body against me.

In my hands I'm holding a doggie seatbelt harness. I have no faith it will make a difference, but in a moment of sheer desperation, I bought it and decided to give it a try. I just can't see anything securing this little white whirling dervish of a dog.

I buckle the purple harness onto Sally with no objections from her. Any kind of a collar or leash means ride to her, so she's happy to oblige. I slide the seatbelt through the strap, and she is secured. She sits in her seat, trembling with excitement.

As we pull out of the driveway and onto the road,

I keep an eye on Sally from the passenger seat. She watches me. A few minutes in and she makes her first move to jump into the front seat. The harness pulls her back. *Whoa!* Surprise flashes through those coal black eyes of hers. She lunges again and is held secure. She does a half turn and looks behind her as if to say, "what is going on back there?" Then she looks back at me, and the staring begins.

I tell Mike to look at her in his rear-view mirror, while I try not to burst with laughter. I don't want to embarrass her, after all. But after watching her continue to lunge, be held secure, wiggle back and then stare at me, I can't hold it any longer and start to giggle.

I am breathing a sigh of relief. Wow! A car ride with Sally, and it is peaceful and safe.

As our ride continues, Mike and I have a conversation that doesn't include phrases like "Sally, get in the back," "Sally, stop stepping on my legs," and "Sally, Sally, Sally." We are interrupted by a sharp little bark from the back seat. The Princess is not happy. I reassure her she is okay and reach back to give her snout a comforting stroke. She isn't having any of it. The rest of the ride consists of barks and a new Sally repertoire that includes strange noises I would only expect to hear from an alien being.

When we arrive at our destination, I am relaxed, happy and have no new scratches or bruises on my arms and legs.

And Sally? I think she is happy, too. At least she is happy to get out of that pretty, purple Sally holder.

What To Do

It is February in Michigan and Mike and I are going to Mexico for a week of sun, sun and more sun. No more popping vitamin D pills like they are Tic Tacs, and instead of the SAD (seasonal affective disorder) light every morning, we will enjoy pure sunshine.

But there is the pet dilemma: What do we do with Mary, Socks, Stan, and of course, Princess Sally? Jake has exams that week so he won't be able to come home. That eliminates one alternative. Now what is left?

1. Take them to one of the great kennels in our area? My boss takes her puppy to a kennel outfitted with a webcam so she can see what he is doing during the day. There are kennels with raised beds in the cages, and some have their very own televisions. I'm not sure what Sally and Mary would want to watch, maybe *Scooby Doo*?

2. Hire a pet sitter? We could hire someone to come in several times per day and let the dogs outside, make sure they have food and water, and play with them.

Of course, the one time I left Sally alone with our mobile pet groomer, Sally hid in the house, and Ingrid couldn't find her.

3. Ask my parents to check on them? Sally is well acquainted with my mom and stepfather, Jim. She has met them hundreds of times. They play with her, talk to her and have, on occasion, let her snuggle on their laps. They have experience taking care of Sally for a day or so. But Jim came over once to let her outside, and she scooted under the bed. Jim got down on his hands and knees and tried coaxing her out with nice words, toys and the ultimate in coaxers, cheese. Nothing worked.

4. Ask my 20-year-old nephew to come stay at the house? Bingo! I call Michel and entice him with a full fridge, use of our car, and the run of the house. It is a done deal.

The week before vacation is spent getting everything ready for our trip. The packing is easy ... bathing

suits. Mary and the cats are easy, but the rest of the preparations, you guessed it, are Sally-focused:

Veterinarian information - This is an important detail since there is always the possibility of an indigestion problem from eating dead, rotting carcasses. Or a pulled neck muscle from obsessively staring at objects for inordinate amounts of time.

Food - I make a special trip to the pet store that sells the specialty dog food. Then I almost dislocate my shoulder carrying the 25 pound bag through the parking lot. When I drop it into the back of the car, there is a large ripping noise and dog food spills into the trunk. Knowing some wayward mouse living in the garage will see this as a buffet, I invite Sally into the car when I get home. She eats too much, which results in throwing up piles of undigested food.

Toys – I buy new bones for Sally and Mary, but can't resist giving it to them right away because Sally is doing her happy spinning dance. She gnaws on it day and night until I take it away because the sound of her teeth grinding is making me batty. She turns her attention to the catnip toy and feigns interest in it until the cats start batting it around. Then she tries to shake it open.

Nighttime rituals – I discuss in detail Sally's nighttime ritual with Michel. Of course, she sleeps in our bed. First, she chews on her bone. When the lights go out, the bone gets put into the bedside table drawer. Sally scoots under the covers to the cave, a spot behind your knees. At this point I think Michel is considering bailing on us, so I hand him the car keys and show him the full freezer.

We call him a few days into the trip.

"Hi Michel, how's it going?"

"Good."

"No problems?"

"Nope."

"How's Sally?"

"Good."

"Where is she sleeping?"

"In bed."

"With you?"

"Under the covers, even."

"You're such a good guy, Michel."

"Yeah, right. Just don't tell anyone."

Oops!

Doggy OCD
aka Obsessive Compulsive Disorder

"Sally, please stop with the water already."

As I arrive home, Sally greets me at the door with her miniature bull terrier exuberance of running into my legs, then spinning in a circle. She follows this with a dash to the water bowl where she begins gulping water like a camel with an empty hump. I call to her and after a few more gulps, she stops and runs back to me for more loving and spinning. Then over to the second water dish where she sticks in her long face, and the gulping starts again. She repeats this act every time Mike or I enter the house. And if we don't call her off this bizarre ritual, she will drink uncontrollably and throw it up. Ugh!

And this is only one in a number of odd Sally rituals.

The spinning is her all-time favorite, and we see it most often when she is happy. So we see it a lot! It consists of her chasing her tail around and around and around. Once she catches it, she will let go so the chasing can continue. I have seen her grab the end of her tail and just stand still, though. She looks like a loop at that point. But if she is really, really happy, then she will just run in a circle, as if she is chasing her tail, but she doesn't try to grab it. And in those circumstances, there might be a few leaps in the air during the spinning. Quite the feat, if you think about it.

Then there is the terrier tear. One evening, my husband Mike and I are in the living room watching TV.

"What is that noise?" I ask.

Mike hits the mute button on the remote and we sit listening. From the bedroom we can hear some Sally sounds, hard to describe on paper, but it is a schnuffling sound. We tiptoe to the bedroom door and peek into the room. Sally is standing at the foot of the bed, panting. Then she tears toward the head of the bed and dives headfirst into the pillows. While still under them, Sally turns and runs back to the foot of the bed. This terrier tear continues for several minutes, back and forth, as we stand with our hands over our mouths, stifling our laughter. Every so often she pauses, pants and then starts again. Pillows are flying, and we have to stop the frivolity when one pillow flies onto the bedside table knocking the lamp and alarm clock onto the floor.

We have also seen the terrier tear repeated on the living room couch. She will tear from one end to the other; blankets, cushions and pillows beware. Once I saw her start the tear while Mary was lying at one end. I think it started because Sally was trying to get Mary to play, but Mary wasn't interested. Sally was doing a little jumping dance at Mary, sort of like "Hey Mary, let's play!" and when Mary jumped off the couch, the tear began.

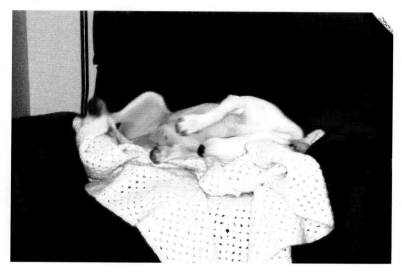

One of the most bizarre Sally rituals is the bedtime face licking. She and I often go to bed before my husband. I'll read for a while, and Sally sits beside me chewing on a toy. It is a very idyllic picture of a mom and her dog enjoying a peaceful evening. That all changes when Mike comes to bed. The toy and my book go into the bedside drawer and we snuggle under the covers. As soon as Mike gets into bed, Sally switches into licking mode. She lunges, really lunges, onto the pillow and starts licking his face.

"What do you think this is about?" he asks one night. It is hard to understand him over the sound of dog saliva being lapped onto his face.

"I have no clue," I mumble. I have my back to the two of them because otherwise Sally's butt will be in my face.

"I'm not going to stop her this time and see how long she does it."

I am gagging from the obsessive licking sound and also from the thought of a dog (yes, even Sally) licking my face for any length of time. I adore Sally, and doggy kisses are fun to get, but this isn't the same. This is obsessive compulsive disorder licking.

"I can't take it anymore," Mike says. "Okay, Sally, that's enough. Come on now. That's enough."

Sally is sitting on the back of my head as Mike pushes her away from his face.

"Ouch, she's pulling my hair," I say.

"Sally, enough with the licking."

"Mike, stop. You're pushing her onto my head."

"Well, she won't quit licking me. Sally, that's enough. Lie down."

"Sally, get your paw out of my ear." I push her leg away and she collapses onto my head. "Mike, a little help would be nice."

Mike gives her a gentle shove toward the foot of the bed; we rearrange the blankets and shut off the lights. I feel Sally's weight as she creeps between us to her favorite sleeping spot.

Then I hear the unmistakable licking noise.

"Sally, come on. Really, that's enough!" Mike says.

I pull the covers over my head.

It's Just A Bowl

It all starts on that fateful day when I make the decision to buy a new bowl set for Sally. It is not a choice taken without due consideration. Standing in the store aisle, I stare at the ceramic set for several minutes. Examining the blue and white bowls with the single paw print in the middle of each, I scrutinize the rubber-coated stand in which the two bowls sit. This will look so much nicer than the single bowl Sally now uses. But would the *I-don't-like-change* little dog use them?

Two years earlier, I had bought a new bowl for her. The old one, a small blue clay dish, she had used since her puppy days, and it was time for a *big girl* bowl. The new one was wider, deeper and multi-colored. I brought it home and at supper time filled it with food and sat it in front of Sally. She backed out of the room, never taking her eye off the villainous bowl. When she got to the bedroom door, she ran to her kennel and dove inside. Mary got the bowl instead.

But this time is going to be different. *Tough love, baby*, I think as I toss, not one, but two of the bowl sets into my cart. One for Mary and the other for the Princess. There is a new sheriff in town, and I am making the decisions, NOT Sally.

At home I gather the old bowls and put them in the dishwasher. I fill one new bowl each with fresh clear water, the other with a cup of food and place the sets on their respective crocheted doggie bone mats. I call the dogs and act like everything is normal. Mary runs to her food and digs in. Sally runs to her food and skids to a stop. She backs up and bumps into the wall.

"Eat your suppies, Sal," I say in a shameless singsong voice. She sticks her long nose out as far as it will go without moving her body and sniffs at the dangerous item.

"Go on Sal, it's okay," I continue. She lifts off her back haunches, without moving her paws, and leans a little farther.

I get down on my hands and knees beside her bowl and grab a handful of food out of her dish. "Here you go Sal. Yum!" Yes, I put the food near my mouth.

She eats a few morsels out of my hand, her body twitching with the exertion of staying a safe distance from the killer bowls. I grab a few more morsels and make a little path from her paws to the bowl. She gobbles the first few pieces, and then she backs up a bit more.

I tap on the bowl. "It's okay, Sal. Really, it's just a bowl." I hold out a few more morsels. The back door opens, and Mike sticks his head into the kitchen. I look up at him with deer-in-the-headlight eyes.

"What are you doing?" he asks, one eyebrow cocked.

"I, uh, bought new bowls. Sally wouldn't eat. I'm … it's pathetic, I know," My shoulders sag as I look at the food in my hand, the food path in front of the dish, and Sally's muscular white body quaking in fear several feet from the bowls.

He shakes his head and backs out of the room.

What happened to the new sheriff in town, I think. I drop the handful of food back into her bowl and stand up.

"Sally, you are going to eat out of that bowl or you're going to go hungry," I say with as much bravado as I can muster. She slinks out of the room and runs to her kennel.

The next morning I put her bowl out and she barks at it. But she doesn't eat out of it. That night, more barking and then a few nibbles. And so on for the next several days. On Saturday, I think we have it made when she eats out of the bowl with no hesitation both morning and night. Same with Sunday and then Monday morning.

Mission accomplished! I held my ground with the little white dog, and she has given in to my bowl exchange. I am elated as I place her evening food dish in front of her. It is good to be the sheriff.

Until she starts barking … at the bowl.

A week later.

"What is that?" Mike asks.

I look around the room, feigning ignorance.

"What is what?"

"That!" He points to Sally who is eating her suppies. "That's her old bowl, isn't it?"

"I couldn't stand it anymore," I whine. "She wouldn't eat and it was becoming a whole … thing!" I throw my arms up in the air for emphasis.

He shakes his head.

"And look how happy she is now," I say.

He shakes his head again.

"Come on, it's just a bowl!" I stammer. Sally burps.

Bugs & Snakes Oh My!

Sally is barking. Only it isn't quite a bark. It is more like a whine/bark. And I know this sound.

"Sally, you just went out. I'm not letting you out again," I call from upstairs. Yes, I talk out loud to my dog. In a house full of pets, I would be crazier if I didn't talk to them.

I know Sally is standing at the front door, right at the bottom of the stairs. I can visualize her standing there, nose to the glass, as she makes her little whine/bark. There are many Sally nose prints on that glass door.

I return to reading and deleting my e-mails while Mary lies sleeping on her pillow beside me. Our cats, Stan and Socks, are vying for the spot on my desk in front of the computer monitor. Socks is distracted by the June bugs, those gross brownish-colored beetles that converge in late spring and buzz around the porch lights. They are banging against the window screen.

I hear the whine/bark again. A little louder this time.

"Sally, come on. You were just outside." Another whine/bark, this one much louder. I sigh and push back my chair. My plan is to stand at the top of the stairs and tell her to chill out. But she isn't at the door, and I continue to hear those odd little noises from her.

I find her in the living room with her front paws on a windowsill, staring at the screen. I hear a little bang and see her head jerk back, then forward again with that whine/bark.

"What are you doing, you crazy little dog?" And then I remember the June bugs. This is the Year of June Bugs for Sally — last year it was the Year of Toads.

I noticed the bugs about two weeks ago when I let Sally out at night. Instead of sprinting into the grass, she made an abrupt stop right outside the front door. There she poked her nose into the corners of the porch and started crunching. Yes, I said crunching. She would scoop those little June bug beetle bodies into her mouth and start munching. It was disgusting! And no amount of gagging from me was dissuading her from her munch fest.

I let her outside and see her jumping and catching the low-flying June bugs out of the air. Jump, *crunch, crunch, crunch.* I am concerned when I see her leap at a big black pinching bug. Lucky for her she missed it. I could imagine her running to the door with a pinching bug hanging from her tongue.

The next day, we are out in the backyard. Sally is playing while I am pulling weeds. Of course, everything

Sally does seems to be playing since that face of hers always looks like she's grinning.

As I walk across the yard, I spot a little garter snake sunning in the grass. I see the snake, and it sees me. Sally does not see it. I point.

"Sally, look. A snake."

She walks toward me and steps on the snake. She stops and looks up at me. The snake is underneath her. He sees her, but she still doesn't see it.

"You dummy," I say and point again. She looks down as the snake curls into a ball. She bends down and the snake strikes at her nose. In a flash Sally's 25-pound muscled body flies straight up in the air like a cartoon

character. When she lands, she leaps back a foot.

Mary comes over to investigate, and the little bitty snake strikes at Mary, too. Both dogs are now circling the snake, trying to sniff it from different directions without being attacked. They are jumpy and twitchy.

Mary paws at the snake, from a foot away, and then lays down beside it. She shows her teeth at Sally as if to say, "This is my snake. Go find your own." Sally stands on the other side of the snake and barks at Mary.

The snake makes its move and heads for the safety of the deck. Sally chases after it. Maybe chase isn't the right word; *moves with great caution toward the snake* is a better description. The snake slides under the deck and Sally digs her long white nose under as far as she can. She snorts dirt. Mary runs back and forth, from one side of the stairs to the other. The rest of the day, whenever I head down the back stairs, Sally is there, ready to be my snake-catcher.

Unless, of course, she is dining on her new cuisine — June Bug Crunch.

Sally's Unique Toy

Multi-colored balls, rubber pork chops, rope-knotted pulls, and furry stuffed shapes line the toy aisle of the pet store. I ponder over the colors, shapes and materials, then grab a pack of bright yellow tennis balls for Mary.

Tennis balls are Mary's favorite toy. You can throw one for hours, and she will bring the ball back, drop it at your feet, and stare until you throw it again. Due to exhaustion, or the increasing slobbery state of the ball, the thrower gives up the game before Mary does.

Tennis balls are also a favorite toy of my niece's dog, Booger. Bull-terrier Scrambles loves to play with empty milk jugs, and German shepherd Griffin, won't let his knotted rope out of his sight. Yet Sally is very particular about her choice of toys.

She prefers a six-foot garden rake. So when shopping for Sally's playthings, go to the hardware store.

The wooden handle of this "toy" is hatched with

serious chew marks and is three times the length of Sally's body. The metal claw-toothed end looks like something out of a horror movie. And this little dog is obsessed with the garden tool.

First, she stares at the rake as it hangs on the wall in our garage. As I carry it into the backyard, Sally runs around me in circles, jumping and spinning and biting at the rake. I sidestep her attempts at tripping me and toss it into the grass.

Craziness ensues.

Sally runs to the rake and makes little *grrrring* noises as she rolls it over and over with her long white snout. She grabs the metal end in her mouth and takes off running across the yard. Often the handle of the rake is between her legs, making it an awkward and slow run. When that happens, she drops the rake, steps alongside it, and grabs it once more. Off she goes, dragging that long garden apparatus beside her.

She has turned rake-running into a talent, too, as she avoids obstacles like trees, flowers and people. Back and forth across the backyard, around the house, and between the gardens, she spends hours with her favorite toy. And as long as we know where the rake is, we know where Sally is.

Until recently.

She has added a new dimension to her rake game. She rolls it, grabs it, then runs into the woods that surround our backyard. At first she would just jog along the edge of the wooded section and then dart back into the yard. Now she has decided to explore this wonderful dense area, while dragging the wooden object behind her.

Twice we have had to enter the mosquito-infested zone, fight our way through saplings, over fallen trees and a flooring of thick leaves, stopping to listen for the sound of her growling at the rake or the jingling of her collar. When we find her she is tugging at the handle because the metal end is stuck in the ground or in a log.

As we carry it back to the yard, Sally only has eyes for her rake. She spins, jumps, and runs in circles, oblivious to the debris under her paws or around her.

During a recent picnic at our house, my son Jake

is throwing Mary's ball when someone asks why poor little Sally doesn't have a ball. We start telling the rake story, then decide it would be easier to just show her obsession. The laughter begins as Jake carries the rake from the garage, and Sally does her circus acrobatics. As soon as he puts the rake on the ground, she grabs it and runs off toward the woods. We round her up, and give her several more opportunities to play with it in the yard.

Doesn't work.

The alternative is to hang the rake from a tree hook that leaves it dangling about two feet off the ground. Sally barks, growls and makes strange yipping noises while attempting to wrestle the rake off the tree. Due to her OCD mania, we know where she will be for the next hour or so.

We set up a badminton game and discover that Sally has a fixation with rackets, too. Go figure! She runs from one racket to the next, back to the rake on the tree, and back to a racket. On and on, back and forth.

At the end of the day, we put the rake back in its spot in the garage. Sally walks forlornly into the house. She jumps onto the bed, curls into a fetal position and begins snoring.

It appears that rake-wrangling is exhausting work.

Princess & the Play Date

Move over Paris Hilton; here comes Princess Sally.

The morning skies are gray, but the weatherman predicts the rain will hold off until evening. Armed with that information, Marianne Evans and I plan our Bull Terrier Play Date. We are excited to introduce Sally to Marianne's Scrambles, a one-year-old, full-size terrier. Marianne had read about Sally in *Cats and Dogs Magazine* and contacted me with the idea of a play date. I am excited!

We arrange to meet at Marianne's friend's house so neither dog will feel territorial about the location. Sally, me and my son Jake, (aka Sally's personal photographer) arrive first. Then several of Scrambles' human relatives show up, and soon the small living room is filled with five humans and one little white bull terrier, excited to share in this bully play. Sally is running from person to person when the front door opens, and Scrambles bolts in. The play date has begun.

At 35-plus pounds, Scrambles outweighs Sally by 10 pounds, but they both have strong muscled bodies.

They do the obligatory sniffing and are off. They chase each other around the small room, knocking into anything in their way, including the legs of tables and humans. I rub my shin where Sally's rock-like head collides with it.

Sally chases Scrambles across the room, then Scrambles chases Sally underneath a coffee table and the closest human grabs the lamp as it wobbles. Saliva flies (from the dogs) as they launch themselves at each other in jubilation. I am guessing at the jubilation. There isn't any growling or blood. So I figure everything is good.

The chasing slows and tongues (again, from the dogs) hang from their mouths. Sally drops at my feet panting, and Scrambles wanders around the room, sniffing everyone.

The dogs are out of breath; the humans look shell-shocked, and the room is starting to smell more and more like dog. Plus, I am concerned about what might happen to the furniture if these maniacs continue their play indoors.

"Let's take them outside," I suggest.

In the chain-linked backyard we set the dogs loose, and they sniff-investigate all the dog toys, trees and plants. Scrambles picks up her favorite toy, an empty milk jug, and shakes it back and forth. We play tug of war.

Then the rain starts.

In dog-like fashion, Scrambles doesn't seem to notice, but Sally is already squinting. Sally doesn't like to get wet. Sally doesn't like water in her eyes. Sally isn't happy.

Since it is only a light sprinkling, we stay outside, not wanting to take two wet dogs back into the house.

Scrambles bangs the muddy milk jug into my leg, as Sally stands at the fence and stares at the back door.

"Come on, Sally," I say. "Let's play."

We are all standing on the concrete pad when my husband, Mike, arrives and tosses Sally's ball into the grass. She starts for it. Scrambles drops the milk jug and the race is on … until Sally steps into the wet grass and slides to a stop. She tippy-toes backward out of the grass.

This is not going well.

Scrambles smacks Sally with her wet milk jug, but Sally steps away. The rain continues. The humans open umbrellas, and I watch my little dog with growing embarrassment. Scrambles is jumping, running, playing and acting like a dog. A very, very energetic dog. Sally is trying to stay under the umbrella.

"I'm going to go wait in the car," Mike says.

"Don't go," I beg.

He shakes his head as he looks at Sally with humiliation, then turns away.

I continue my hope that the play date will turn out well with Sally interacting with Scrambles. I keep on urging Sally to play. But no, she has decided she is done. I hold an umbrella over Jake as he attempts to take photos of the *fun and frivolity*. But the Princess doesn't work in the rain. There is no fun, and certainly no frivolity.

"Maybe we should try a drier day," I say.

Agreement among the humans is quick and overwhelming. I give Scrambles a hug, thank Marianne, and pick up Sally.

As she burrows her nose under my arm, I can't help but give my little diva a kiss on her long sloping damp forehead.

The Night Sniffer

Some *thing* is licking my forehead. I open one eye and peek at the clock. It is 4:38 a.m. I lie still, hoping Sally, the some *thing*, will forego the need to go outside. This is the third time since midnight I have awoken to her wet tongue sliding over my face. The licking stops and I feel her muscular body wiggle under the blankets and burrow into the space behind my knees. I sigh, the blankets fly into the air, and Sally leaps back onto my pillow.

"You win, Sally," I say. She bounds across the bed and leaps onto the floor. I grab my glasses and swing my legs out of bed. I step over Mary, who is snuggled in pillows on the floor. She doesn't stir.

Sally leads the way, and I stumble through the kitchen. After I open the door, she scoots between my legs, across the porch and down the stairs. The night sky is brightened by a full moon, and I step onto the deck, rough wood scratching my bare feet. Sally is sniffing

139

lavender bushes, mole tunnels, and the spot where she peed two hours ago.

"Sally, take care of business," I remind her. She glances at me and squats. My guess is that it is just an obligatory squat since this is the third time in four hours. I turn toward the door, and out of the corner of my eye I see something hop in the grass. A toad! Should the little white dog see this, it will result in a huge delay in getting her back into the house.

Sally is now examining a hollow log near the fire pit. I hurry away from the toad-object-of-distraction and

call her. She buries her nose farther into the log.

"You little snot," I say. Stepping off the stairs, my feet sink into the coolness of the lush grass. I wiggle my toes, and they seem to sigh with relief after the sharpness of the deck. I head toward the wood pile.

"Sally!" She jumps backward, tripping on a pile of branches. "Get in that house." I point toward the main stairs, hoping to herd her away from the toad. She darts up the stairs and through the open door. By the time I get to the bedroom, she is curled on Mike's pillow. He is gone this week. Perhaps his first night away is the reason for Sally's restlessness.

The next day I weed my flower gardens, then read a book in the hammock. Sally drags her rake around the yard, spins with happiness, and visits me at the hammock for an occasional ear rub. Mary lounges, following the sunshine as it moves to different locations on the deck.

By evening I have finished my book and moved inside to the recliner. I zone out watching television. Mary is snoring on the couch. Sally is curled on my lap after an exhausting day with her rake. At 10:30 p.m., I suggest we go to bed, and she dashes to the door. We always let her out before we go to bed, thinking it will diminish her need to go during the night. Sometimes it works. Sometimes, like last night, it doesn't. I let her outside and then wander to the bathroom.

When I return to the door, Sally is not waiting to come in. It's not that unusual, and I'm not worried, yet, because I know she is nearby. I brush my teeth and change into my pajamas, anticipating she will be waiting at the door when I return. Still, no Sally.

Now a wee bit worried, I walk onto the porch and look around for her ghostly white body. Nothing. That is unusual.

Our house is on a secluded road with no street-lights, so I grab a flashlight. Wandering around the driveway I flash it into the wooded areas surrounding the house. I still don't see my little princess. I stand and listen for her movements. Nothing.

So here I am, standing in my driveway in complete darkness, wearing my pajamas. And I have spent the last two hours watching the investigation of grisly murders on *Forensic Files*. My imagination leaps into high gear. Even though I don't hear dog noises, I hear sounds that could be the murderer from California who stabbed a woman 101 times. After all, they never found him, and since the episode was from 2006, he has had plenty of time to travel across the country and find my backyard. Or maybe it is the serial killer who attacks after women let their dogs outside at night. Brandishing the flashlight like a weapon, I back toward the house. Adrenaline is coursing through my veins, and my heart palpitates. I move with deliberate, quick steps until I am safe in the house.

Still no Sally. What if there is a stalker of miniature bull terriers named Sally loose in the woods?

I take a few deep breaths, then walk back onto the porch. Rather than return to the driveway, I move to the end of the porch and look around.

There! My flashlight beam picks up a pair of beady black eyes. Sally! She is frozen in front of the water hose. She looks up at me, back to the ground, up at me, and back to the ground. I follow her gaze, and there on the concrete is a toad. While I was confronting imagined killers and regaining my bravery, Sally was having a stare down with a toad.

I would have laughed, but for the sound of the *Forensic Files* music wafting from the television.

Exercise Is For Turkeys

Sally and I have become potatoes. I can't really say *couch* potatoes, more like *recliner* potatoes or *bed* potatoes.

My day starts when I open my eyes to see a little white snout facing me on my pillow. The face grins at me. At least it seems to be grinning from that close proximity, and then it breaks into a yawn that emits awful doggy morning breath.

I look past the furry face to my husband Mike's pillow, and see a sleep-apnea masked head. It is like sleeping with Darth Vader. Fur or mask, it can be a frightening way to start my day.

I roll out of bed and let Sally and Mary outside. Mary runs into the woods to take care of her business. Sally walks about two feet from the door, squats, and then scampers back to the house. If there is dew on the grass, she only moves one foot from the door into the soil surrounding the porch. God forbid the princess gets her paws wet.

My body movement at this point is to lean against the doorframe and yawn.

Back in the house, Mary runs in a circle through the living room and down the hallway several times. Sally trots to the bedroom, leaps onto bed and wiggles underneath the covers.

I go into the bathroom, drag the scale out from the closet where it was thrown unhappily the day before, and step on it. Then I step off, thinking it is broken, give it another chance and step back on. The digital numbers blink higher each time.

It is time to make some changes. So armed with the enthusiasm of a New Year's resolution maker on January 1, I decide we will start each day with an invigorating walk. Starting tomorrow!

The next morning I give the sleeping snout a little kiss, and then I jump out of bed. My unexpected fast movement causes the room to start spinning, so I plop back down, somehow managing to sit on Sally. She leaps backwards, landing on Darth Vader.

"What are you doing?" the muffled voice behind the mask asks.

"Going for a walk with the dogs. Wanna come?" I dress in my new periwinkle blue exercise outfit and matching headband.

A hiss emanates from the mask and I take that as a no.

Sitting up from tying my shoes, I try to catch my breath. I am going to have to find a pair of slip-on walking shoes.

Outside, the air is crisp as the dogs and I head down the driveway. I am prepared to make six trips back and forth down the long lane. Mary takes off like a shot, and Sally chases her, herding her off the road and along the edge of the woods. I smile and marvel at the changing colors of the leaves on the trees. I hear the gobbling of wild turkeys in the woods, but I am not concerned, knowing Mary is too deaf to hear them and Sally, if she saw them, would hide behind my legs. She is not the guard dog type.

Before I know it, we are ending the second leg of our new morning journey, and I am not even tired. I have visions of pulling up my jeans and actually buttoning them. And the form-fitting sweater thrown under the bed? It's coming out, baby! *Fit and trim,* that is my new motto. Look out washboard ab models, here comes your competition!

Heading into the third round, Mary bounds ahead, but Sally stops and looks back at the house with longing.

"Come on, Sal," I say. "We can do this."

She trudges along behind, her pace slowing considerably. I keep looking back to make sure she is following, and each time she slows even more. I feel a bump against the back of my legs. I look down and see her poking my calf with her snout. Is she trying to trip me?

By the fourth turn on our lane, I'm begging Sally to keep up. Only three more lengths to go. But now my legs are burning, and it feels like the dirt road has turned into wet cement. Those models I'm picturing in my mind are looking less attractive, and as long as the zipper works, is it really necessary to button jeans? And that sweater under the bed? It's too covered in dust bunnies to wear anyway.

And really, as a conscientious pet owner, isn't it important that I don't exhaust poor little Sally?

I bend down and pat her head just as a lone turkey, hiding in the bushes about a foot from us, leaps into the air. I stumble backwards, and Mary jumps on me. All I see of Sally are little dust funnels in her wake as she hightails it to the house.

That night, I turn off the alarm setting.

"What happened to the morning walks?" the mask asks.

"A maniacal turkey attached us this morning." I crawl into bed, and Sally snuggles into the cave behind my knees. "It is just too dangerous out there."

I choose to ignore the muffled mask laughter.

Not So Much

The bedroom sheers dance with each wind gust. Lying in bed, I listen to the branches bending and creaking. I love windy nights. Sally ... not so much.

Under the covers, Sally is snuggled close to my legs, as if she has been super-glued to my body. She breaks free and pokes her head out from under the blanket. The curtains move. She scrambles back underneath. The wind calms. She's back, and this time she makes it all the way to the pillow.

She stands on my head, staring at the window. "Sally, move," I say into her belly fur. I give her a little shove, and she falls onto my husband's arm.

"What?" Mike mumbles in his sleep. The wind gusts and she sprints across my body.

"Ow!" I clutch at my belly.

"What?" Mike asks again.

"She just ..." I hear him snoring.

Sally runs back and licks my face, code for going outside.

"Really?" I groan. "Now?"

"What?" Mike says. This time he may be talking in his sleep.

I step over Mary, sleeping on pillows next to the bed, as Sally and I head through the house. She cowers behind my legs as the wind whistles through open windows. At the door, she bolts down the steps and into the grass. The woods are alive with branches bending, leaves swirling and bushes rustling. Sally stands with her nose up, sniffing the turbulent air. She doesn't seem afraid outside. I feel an energy in the night air, lift my head and sniff, too. Sally squats. Uh, time to stop sniffing.

A gust grabs the picnic table umbrella, lifts it off the deck and drops it onto the grass. Open, it bounces like a huge tumbleweed toward the little squatting dog. Sally dashes away from the umbrella, while I run toward it.

Barefoot and in my pajamas, I am pursuing a big red umbrella that's chasing a little white dog.

The wind picks up, and as I grab the end of the umbrella, I struggle to get it closed. Small twigs fly through the air as I prop it next to the house.

Sally has stopped running and watches me from the edge of the woods, panting. A branch cracks behind her, and she dashes to the house, never looking back. The door bangs, and she skids to a stop at the bottom of the stairs. I scoop her up and hurry into the house.

The wind no longer whistles through the open windows. It howls. The curtains no longer dance, they twist and jerk like agitated ghosts. I put Sally down and she watches the mayhem as I rush around closing windows.

In the bedroom the sheers are blowing, but the wind has created a nice cool room for sleep. I feel my way through the dark to the bed and lay down ... on top of Sally. She wiggles out from under me and leaps across Mike's body.

"What?" he says.

I lie down, and Sally snuggles beside me. A gust of wind rattles the window, and she stands on full alert. Then back down. Then back up. With each move she bumps against Mike's arm or worse, his head. I coax her to lie on the other side of me. Up, down. She repeats the pattern. This is so not working.

At this rate, no human or canine is going to get any sleep, and Mike has an early morning. I grab my pillow and head upstairs to the guest room. Sally dashes up the stairs ahead of me and waits at the door, her butt wiggling. The wind howls until I close and latch all the windows.

Quiet.

I am wide awake. Sally slips under the covers, turns and lays her head on the pillow. Within minutes she is sleeping.

I listen to the tapping of raindrops on the window and Sally's steady breathing beside me. There is a muffled rumble of thunder, and I burrow into the blankets. As I drift off to sleep, I hear the click click click of doggy toenails on the hardwood floor.

I love thunderstorms. Mary, well, not so much .

Prologue

When I started writing my Life With Sally column for *Cats and Dogs* magazine, I thought I'd run out of story ideas at some point. Well, that point never arrived.

Silly Sally continues to provide me with writing material, including her antics during our vacation this past summer, which included a nine-hour drive, and her birthday in October, replete with party hats and cake. Plus, I just signed her up for Doga ... yoga with your dog. I can't wait to see how Sally pulls off the downward

canine position. (Fortunately, she's already close to the floor).

And snow in Michigan means the return of the snow shovel, which means the return of one of Sally's winter obsessions, dragging the shovel around our yard.

If you have any suggestions for a Sally story, please visit my website at www.awritingpassage.com and leave a message. I would really love to hear from you.

~Tricia

Life With Sally
Little White Dog Tails

Books may be ordered online at

www.awritingpassage.com

or by mail at

Writing Avenue, LLC
17190 Van Wagoner Road
Spring Lake, MI 49456

$13.95 + $2.99 shipping

Your copy will be autographed by
Tricia and Sally.